The Daily Telegraph
Tax Guide 2016

The Daily Telegraph
Tax Guide 2016

Understanding the tax system, completing your tax return and planning how to become more tax efficient

David Genders

KoganPage

LONDON PHILADELPHIA NEW DELHI

First published as *The Daily Telegraph Guide to Income Tax, 1974* by Constable & Robinson Ltd
This edition published in Great Britain in 2016 by Kogan Page Limited

2nd Floor, 45 Gee Street
London EC1V 3RS
United Kingdom
www.koganpage.com

© Telegraph Media Group, 2016

The right of David Genders to be identified as the author of this work has been asserted by him in accordance with the Copyright, Designs and Patents Act 1988.

ISBN   978 0 7494 7679 3
E-ISBN   978 0 7494 7690 8

British Library Cataloguing-in-Publication Data

A CIP record for this book is available from the British Library.

Typeset by Graphicraft Limited, Hong Kong
Print production managed by Jellyfish
Printed and bound by CPI Group (UK) Ltd, Croydon CR0 4YY

CONTENTS

18   Budget measures   248

Appendices 259

ABOUT THE AUTHOR

David Genders has been writing *The Daily Telegraph Tax Guide* since 1982. A former partner of Sayers Butterworth LLP, Chartered Accountants in London, he joined the firm in 1965 as an apprentice before qualifying as a chartered accountant in 1970. After a career specializing in taxation, focusing on personal tax, David retired from his position of senior partner seven years ago. He has, however, been retained by the practice as a tax consultant. David brings a wealth of knowledge and experience to this guide.

Away from tax affairs, David enjoys bridge, golf, gardening and walking. Regular readers of the guide will know that for many years David harboured an ambition to drive a steam train. This goal was achieved in 2014 on the North Yorkshire Moors Railway between Grossmont and Pickering. A day to be long remembered. His next challenge is to get his handicap at golf under 20!

Introduction

We all want a better education for our children, an improved National Health Service, a more efficient and reliable transport system, less congestion on the roads and to feel safer and more secure in our homes and when we walk the streets. So who has to foot the bill for all these services? The Government, of course. And how does the Government raise the revenues to meet this expenditure? Mainly by taxing income, wealth, production and imports as well as collecting social contributions from us. Any deficit from one year to the next is funded by borrowing.

The taxes covered in this guide are:

- Income Tax – what we pay annually on our earnings and income from savings.
- Capital Gains Tax – paid only when we realize profits on sales of our assets.
- Inheritance Tax – chargeable on some lifetime gifts of capital and on the value of our estates on death.
- Value Added Tax – included in the price of many goods and services we buy.
- National Insurance and Social Security – the contributions we have to pay based on our earnings or business profits and the various benefits, including the State Pension, we receive in return.
- Tax credits – whether you are eligible and how to work out what you can claim.

For many people tax is both confusing and complicated. This book aims to:

- explain the basics of the taxes covered for the average taxpayer as straightforwardly as possible;
- help readers have a better understanding of their tax affairs and, therefore, be able to take control;

- make staying within the law as easy as possible; and
- help cut tax bills with pointers to saving on tax.

This edition of *The Daily Telegraph Tax Guide* is primarily intended to cover the Self Assessment tax year from 6 April 2015 to 5 April 2016 and is being published soon after you should have received a Tax Return for this year.

The tax changes announced by the Chancellor of the Exchequer in his 2015 July Budget and Autumn Statement, as well as the 2016 March Budget, are set out in the final chapter of the book.

I hope you benefit from the read.

You and HMRC

Ask any taxpayer the question 'Would you like to pay less tax?' and I imagine that, almost without exception, the answer would be 'Yes'. By the time you have finished reading this book I would like to think that you will have come across at least one way of saving tax. Maybe:

- another allowance or relief you can claim;
- an expense that could be included in your business accounts; or
- a more tax-efficient structuring of your cash savings and investments.

But, first of all, you should have an understanding of the workings of the various HM Revenue & Customs (HMRC) departments responsible for the day-to-day running of our tax system.

The board of HMRC has overall authority for administering the fiscal legislation enacted by Government. Although there are a large number of specialist departments within HMRC, it is likely that your only contact with it will be through the staff at your tax office and the accounts offices.

Tax offices

Each tax office throughout the country is headed up by a senior officer with a full support staff. The tax affairs of employees and pensioners are looked after by the tax office that deals with the Pay-As-You-Earn affairs of their employer or pension fund. If you are self-employed you may find that the tax office responsible for your tax affairs is sometimes local to your business address.

It is your service office that:

- sends you a Tax Return to complete each year;
- processes your Return when you send it back;
- corrects any obvious or simple errors that you have made and sends you a notice detailing the amendments; and

- initially chases you up if you are late sending in your Return. Service offices are also responsible for:
  - looking after all the day-to-day tax matters of the vast majority of taxpayers whose income is taxed under Pay-As-You-Earn and do not come within the system of Self Assessment; and
  - processing the business accounts of self-employed taxpayers.

As long as you comply with all your tax obligations in a timely manner, your only involvement with HMRC will be confined to your service office.

Wealthy taxpayers

If you are one of the wealthiest taxpayers your tax affairs are looked after by the High Net Worth Unit (HNWU). It is intended that the HNWU will:

- build relationships to help better understand these taxpayers and make it easier for them to get things right; and
- better tailor service delivery for these taxpayers through proactive engagement and by providing a single point of contact as well as a holistic approach for their tax affairs.

High-earning taxpayers whose affairs are otherwise largely uncomplicated are dealt with by an HMRC office in Stockton-on-Tees.

Taxpayers with particular needs

HMRC offer a range of facilities for taxpayers with particular needs; for example, if:

- you are blind or partially sighted;
- you are deaf, have impaired hearing or have a speech impediment; or
- your first language is not English.

If you think you need extra help, the number to call is 0300 200 3300.

Accounts offices

The main tasks of HMRC accounts offices are to:

- bank payments of tax and National Insurance Contributions; and
- keep up-to-date, accurate payments records.

If you need to telephone, write to or visit any of these offices, always give your name and reference number. You can find the address and telephone number on forms and letters that have been sent to you.

Dealing with HMRC

The following services are available to you by telephoning 0300 200 3300:

- personal information such as changes of address or in your personal circumstances;
- employment details;
- claims to personal allowances;
- claims for either tax relief on flat-rate expenses (see Appendix 2 on pages 261–62) or certain professional subscriptions to be included in the PAYE coding for the current year;
- employee benefits such as a company car, fuel for private motoring and medical insurance that affect your PAYE coding;
- notification of Gift Aid payments or contributions into your pension plan;
- savings and investment income;
- State and other pensions;
- taxable State benefits;
- income from renting out your home when you are away from it;
- income from letting out a room in your home;
- other property income;
- making certain amendments to your Self Assessment Return; and
- dealing with tax repayments due to you.

In most cases nothing more will be needed from you, although the call may lead to further action by HMRC (for example, sending out a revised PAYE Coding Notice). Where your business cannot be completely dealt with by telephone, the HMRC officer will arrange to send you any necessary forms or follow-up material.

When you telephone do not be put off by any steps taken to establish your identity. Any such checks are for the purpose of safeguarding the privacy of your tax affairs.

On any matter that does not come within the 'business by telephone' services, I recommend you put any questions in writing to HMRC at: Pay as You Earn and Self Assessment, HM Revenue & Customs, BX9 1AS.

Whenever you telephone or write always remember to quote your reference number, which is:

- your employer's PAYE reference; or

- your National Insurance Number; or

- if you are self-employed or pay tax at the higher rate, your Self Assessment Unique Taxpayer Reference (UTR). This is a 10-digit number.

Compliance checks and enquiries

Once your Return has been processed by your tax office, it will undergo a comprehensive programme of checks. Any obvious errors, for example in your arithmetic, will be corrected. Alternatively, HMRC will write or telephone to resolve any queries relating to:

- your Self Assessment Tax Return;

- your accounts and tax calculations; and

- the taxes you pay.

In most cases, no further questions will be asked. But enquiries will be started by your tax office if:

- something requires fuller explanation;

- there is a risk your Return may be incorrect; or

- your Return is selected for enquiry at random.

Normally, HMRC have 12 months from the date that your Return is received by your tax office in which to tell you that it will be the subject of enquiries. However, the time limits for paper and online Returns differ slightly as illustrated by the following table for 2015/16 Returns.

When filed	Enquiry window
Paper Returns	
On time – by 31 October 2016	12 months from the day the Return was filed.
Filed late	Up to, and including, the quarter day following the first anniversary of the date of filing the Return.
Online Returns	
On time – by 31 January 2017	12 months from the day the Return was filed.
Filed late	Up to, and including, the quarter day following the first anniversary of the date of filing the Return.

Your Return will normally become final if your tax office has not raised any enquiries within the permitted time period. HMRC can only raise enquiries at a later date if they discover an error that they could not reasonably have been expected to be aware of from the information provided in, or with, your Return.

At the end of an enquiry into your Return HMRC will issue a closure notice, which will include the making of any necessary adjustments to your Self Assessment. You have 30 days in which to appeal against such amendments.

Any enquiries by your tax office should be conducted in accordance with the specific code of practice laid down by HMRC. If your Tax Return ever becomes the subject of an enquiry, this may well be a time when you should be represented by a professional tax adviser.

Determinations

Not surprisingly HMRC has special powers to deal with taxpayers who are sent a Return but fail to complete it and submit it by the filing date. In such cases an offending taxpayer can expect HMRC to make a determination of his or her income and capital gains chargeable to tax to the best of their knowledge and belief. The actual amount of tax is based on estimates of:

- the taxpayer's allowances and reliefs; and
- tax deducted at source on earnings and savings income.

Any determination can be subsequently superseded by a Self Assessment by the taxpayer or HMRC based on information provided by the taxpayer.

Assessments and appeals

In cases of fraud or neglect your Inspector of Taxes can raise an assessment to collect tax that should have been paid on a Self Assessment.

You do, of course, have a right of appeal against:

- an assessment raised by your Tax Inspector; or
- an amendment to your Return following an enquiry.

The procedure for resolving your appeal starts with a hearing before an independent tribunal of expert tax judges and/or panel members. It can then move on to the courts and ultimately to the House of Lords.

Prosecutions

An important role of HMRC is to deter fraud. They will prosecute in serious cases in all areas of the tax system. Cases selected for prosecution involve a wide range of offences. However, a case is more likely to be considered for prosecution if it contains features such as:

- falsification of documents;
- lying during an investigation;
- conspiracy; or
- discovery of false documents made during an earlier investigation.

Your Charter

HMRC make sure that money is available to fund the UK Public Services by collecting the taxes and duties as laid down by Parliament.

HMRC want to:

- give you a service that is even-handed, accurate and based on mutual trust and respect; and
- make it as easy as they can for you to get things right.

This Charter explains what you can expect from HMRC and what HMRC can expect from you.

Your rights

What you can expect from HMRC:

Respect you

HMRC will:

- treat you with courtesy and consideration;
- listen to your concerns;
- answer your questions in a way you can understand;
- try to understand your circumstances;
- make you aware of your rights, including your right to appeal their decisions; and
- tell you how to exercise your right to appeal against their decisions.

Help and support you to get things right

HMRC will:

- provide information that helps you to understand what you have to do and when you have to do it;
- provide information that clearly explains the taxes, duties, exemptions, allowances, reliefs and tax credits that they are responsible for;
- process the information you give them as quickly and accurately as they can; and
- put mistakes right as soon as they can.

Treat you as honest

Unless HMRC have a good reason not to, they will:

- presume you are telling them the truth;
- accept that you will pay what you owe and only claim what you are entitled to;

- explain why they need to ask you questions and why they have decided to check your records; and
- only question what you tell them if they have good reason to.

Treat you even-handedly

HMRC will:

- act within the law and their published guidance;
- help you understand your legal rights;
- explain what you can do if you disagree with their decisions or want to make a complaint;
- provide you with information in a way that meets your particular needs; and
- consider any financial difficulties you may be having.

Be professional and act with integrity

HMRC will:

- act with integrity;
- make sure that you are dealt with by people who have the right level of expertise;
- make decisions in accordance with the law and published guidance and explain these decisions clearly to you;
- respond to your enquiries and resolve any problems as soon as they can; and
- let you know how appeals, investigations or complaints are progressing.

Tackle people who deliberately break the rules and challenge those who bend the rules

HMRC will:

- identify people who are not paying what they owe or claiming more than they should;
- recover the money they owe and charge interest and penalties where appropriate;
- distinguish between legitimately trying to pay the lowest amount and bending rules through tax avoidance; and
- use their powers reasonably.

Protect your information and respect your privacy

HMRC will:

- protect information they obtain, receive or hold about you;
- explain why they need information, if you ask them to;
- only allow their staff to see information when they need it to do their job;
- give you the information they hold about you when you ask for it, as long as the law lets them;
- only share or release information about you when the law lets them and they need to; and
- respect your legal rights when they visit premises.

Accept that someone else can represent you

HMRC will:

- respect your representative's right to act for you and deal with them appropriately.

Do all they can to keep the cost of dealing with them as low as possible

HMRC will:

- try to make their services straightforward and easy to access;
- make it as cheap as they can for you to contact them;
- explain clearly what they need from you;
- do their best to give you complete, accurate and consistent advice; and
- do their best to get things right first time.

Your obligations

What HMRC expect from you:

Be honest

HMRC expect you to:

- be truthful, open and act within the law;
- give them accurate information;

- give them all the relevant facts; and
- tell them as soon as you can if you think you have made a mistake.

Respect their staff

HMRC expect you to:

- be polite; and
- accept that they will not tolerate rude or abusive behaviour.

Take care to get things right

HMRC expect you to:

- take reasonable care when you complete tax returns and fill out forms;
- send them tax returns and forms on time;
- make payments on time;
- respond in good time if they ask you to do something;
- talk to them if there is anything that you are not sure about or if you are having difficulty meeting your obligations;
- tell them if you have any particular needs so they can take them into account;
- tell them about any changes in your circumstances that will affect your payments or claims; and
- keep adequate records that support what you tell them and hold them for as long as the law says you need to.

Complaints

Any complaint should, first of all, be made to the tax office with which you are dealing, either by telephone or in writing. Address your letter to the Officer in Charge:

- describe the complaint (for example, slow service, constant mistakes); and
- what went wrong and when it happened.

Most complaints about HMRC's handling of people's tax affairs are satisfactorily settled by their tax office. Where taxpayers are not satisfied with the response from their office, they can take their case to a different complaints handler.

Taxpayers who are still dissatisfied can put their case to the HMRC Adjudicator, who will consider complaints about the way in which HMRC:

- have handled their tax affairs – for example, complaints about excessive delay, errors, discourtesy; or
- have exercised discretion.

The Adjudicator will review all the facts and try to reach a decision as soon as possible. HMRC normally accept this decision except where there are exceptional circumstances.

Taxpayers can also ask a Member of Parliament to refer their complaint to the Parliamentary and Health Service Ombudsman. The Ombudsman, who is independent, will look into a complaint, but usually after it has first of all been considered by the Adjudicator.

Changes in legislation

Every year in March or early April the Chancellor of the Exchequer makes his annual Budget Statement. This is often preceded by a Pre-Budget Report, usually in the previous November or December. Not only does he use these occasions to report on the nation's finances, but he also tells us about:

- tax rates and allowances for the following year; and
- new or amending legislation to our tax laws.

Resulting legislative changes are published in a Finance Bill. Its various clauses are debated by Parliament and occasionally amended. Subsequently, the Bill is passed by both Houses of Parliament before receiving Royal Assent. It is then published as a Finance Act.

When the law is either unclear or ambiguous HMRC will issue a Statement of Practice indicating how they intend to interpret it. There are also times when HMRC do not seek to go by the strict letter of the law. These are gathered together and published as a list of Extra-Statutory Concessions.

Tax rates and allowances

For most of us our annual tax bill is determined by:

- tax bands and rates; and
- the allowances we can claim.

Income Tax rates

Under our tax system, the tax (or fiscal) year runs from each 6 April to the following 5 April.

The rates of tax for 2015/16 are:

Band of taxable income (£)	Rate of tax (%)	Tax on band (£)	Cumulative tax (£)
0–31,785	20	6,357.00	6,357.00
31,786–150,000	40	47,286.00	53,643.00
over 150,000	45		

The rates of 20 per cent and 40 per cent are respectively known as the basic and higher rates. The additional rate refers to tax at the 45 per cent level.

Income from dividends is taxed at:

- 10 per cent on dividend income within the basic rate limit of £31,785;
- 32.5 per cent within the higher rate tax band; and
- 37.5 per cent above the higher rate limit.

Savings income

Savings income is that such as interest on a bank or building society account. It does not include dividends on your stocks and shares.

Tax Saver

No tax is charged on your savings income:

- of up to £5,000; but
- after taking off your tax allowances.

To get all the interest on your savings income tax free in 2015/16, your taxable income for the year should usually not exceed £15,600, comprising:

- your personal allowance of £10,600;
- plus £5,000.

But it can be more if you are entitled to other allowances, such as:

- the age-related personal allowance;
- the relief given to a registered blind person;
- the married couple's allowance; and
- the new transferable marriage tax allowance.

However, because earnings and pensions are treated as the first slice of taxable income not all taxpayers will benefit from this nil tax rate on savings income.

Florence Kirk earned £14,000 and had savings income of £3,000 during 2015/16. She paid Income Tax of £960.00 calculated as follows:

	£
Total Income	17,000
Less: Personal allowance	10,600
Taxable Income	6,400
Income Tax payable	**£**
£1,600 @ 0 per cent	Nil
£4,800 @ 20 per cent	960.00
	£462.00

Florence's personal allowance is first of all set against earnings of £14,000, which restricts the amount of her savings income taxable at 0 per cent by £3,400.

Allowances

The amount of your personal allowance depends on:

- your date of birth; and
- your taxable income from all sources.

The rates of the various tax allowances for 2015/16 are:

	£
Personal	
born after 5 April 1948	10,600*
born between 6 April 1938 and 5 April 1948	10,600*
born before 6 April 1938	10,660**
Marriage	
both spouse / partner born after 5 April 1935	1,060***
Married couples	
either spouse / partner born before 6 April 1935	8,355**/****
minimum amount	3,220***
Relief for blind person (each)	2,290

*   the personal allowance reduces at the rate of £1 for every £2 of income in excess of £100,000.
**   these personal and married couple's allowances come down by £1 for every £2 of income above
        a specified limit – £27,700 for 2015/16.
*** transferable to your husband, wife or civil partner. Neither spouse nor civil partner must pay
        tax above the basic rate.
**** indicates where tax relief is restricted to 10 per cent.

In working out the amount of Income Tax payable each year:

- the personal, blind person's and transferred marriage allowances are taken off total income; and
- tax relief for the married couple's allowance is given as a deduction from tax payable.

Indexation

Unless Parliament decides otherwise most allowances and the tax rate bands are linked to annual inflation increases. This movement is in line with the increase in the Retail Prices Index (RPI) during the year to the end of September prior to the tax year and applies to:

- the married couple's allowance;
- blind person's relief; and
- the income limit for age-related allowances.

Personal allowance

Every man, woman or child, single or married and resident in the United Kingdom can claim the personal allowance. This is set against total taxable income from all sources, such as:

- a wage, salary or business profits;
- an occupational and/or a State Pension;
- interest on savings;
- income from investments; and
- rental income.

During 2015/16, Richard West, a married man in his early 40s, earned £34,600 from his job. His tax liability for the year is £4,800.00, worked out as follows:

Remuneration	£
Salary	34,600
Less: Personal allowance	10,600
Taxable income	24,000
Income Tax payable	
£24,000 @ 20 per cent	£4,800.00

Paul Frost received remuneration, including benefits, of £108,000 during 2015/16. His tax liability for the year amounted to £34,203.00, worked out as follows:

	£
Remuneration	108,000
Less: Personal allowance	6,600
Taxable income	101,400
Income Tax payable	
£31,785 @ 20 per cent	6,357.00
£69,615 @ 40 per cent	27,846.00
	£34,203.00

Paul's personal allowance for the year is reduced by £4,000 (1/2 x £108,000 – £100,000) from £10,600 to £6,600.

Tax Saver

The marginal rate of tax on income in the band from £100,000 to £121,000 is 60 per cent or 37.5 per cent on net dividends! If your net income is somewhere in this band the payment of:

- Gift Aid donations (see Chapter 4); and/or
- allowable pension contributions (see Chapter 9),

is very tax efficient.

As the table on page 16 shows, the amount of your annual personal allowance depends on your age. A taxpayer who was born before 6 April 1938 receives a higher personal allowance.

Marriage allowance

New for 2015/16 is the marriage allowance, which you can claim if all of the following requirements apply:

- you are married or in a civil partnership;
- both of you were born after 5 April 1935;
- your income for 2015/16 is not more than £10,600, plus up to £5,000 of tax-free savings interest; and
- your spouse or partner's income for 2015/16 is between £10,601 and £42,385.

Tax Saver

The marriage allowance enables you to transfer £1,060 of your 2015/16 personal allowance to your spouse or partner. By so doing you will save tax of £212 for the year (£1,060 @ 20%).

Clearly it is only advantageous to claim the marriage allowance in cases where one spouse or civil partner is unable to claim all or part of their personal allowance because of a low income.

You can apply for the marriage allowance by registering online at **www.gov.uk/marriage-allowance**. If your application is accepted, the changes to your own and your spouse's/partner's personal allowances will be backdated to the beginning of the tax year.

If you or your spouse/partner were born before 6 April 1935 you may be able to claim the married couple's allowance (see below).

Other features of this new measure are:

- The allowance is transferable in full or not at all.
- In years subsequent to 2015/16 it will be equivalent to 10 per cent of the basic personal allowance.

Married couple's allowance

You can claim the married couple's allowance if you can satisfy all of the following:

- you are married or in a civil partnership;
- one of you was born before 6 April 1935; and
- you are living together.

It is the husband's income which is used to calculate the married couple's allowance for a couple married before 5 December 2005. For marriage and civil partnerships after this date it is the person with the higher income.

Tax Saver

For 2015/16 the married couple's allowance could lower your tax bill from anywhere between £322 and £835.50.

Tax Saver

For some reason you may not be able to live with your spouse or civil partner. This may be because:

- a spouse or partner needs to be in residential care owing to illness or old age;
- your job takes you away from home;
- you are in education or training; or
- you are in prison.

When you are living apart through any of these circumstances you can still claim the married couple's allowance.

Eric Black was 83 years old in 2015/16. His younger wife, Myra, celebrated her 64th birthday the same year. They are entitled to allowances of £19,015 and £10,600 as follows:

	Eric (£)	Myra (£)
Personal age/personal allowance	10,660	10,600
Married couple's allowance	8,355	
Total allowances	19,015	10,600

Long-standing partners Rex Gardner and Gerald Sullivan entered into a Civil Partnership on 4 January 2015. They are both in their mid-80s. Gerald, who has the higher income, can claim the married couple's allowance of £8,355 for 2015/16.

The amount of the married couple's allowance in the year of marriage:

- depends upon the time in the year that the wedding takes place; and
- is reduced by one-twelfth for every complete month from 6 April up to the day of the marriage.

Percy Hughes, aged 85, married his wife, Barbara, aged 67, on 7 November 2015. He receives an allowance of £3,482 for 2015/16 worked out as follows:

	£
Married couple's allowance	8,355
Less: Reduction	
7/12 × £8,355	4,873
2015/16 Allowance	3,482

There is no reduction in the married couple's allowance for a year when:

- couples separate;
- couples divorce; or
- one spouse dies (a widow is entitled to any unused part of the married couple's allowance for the year in which she loses her husband).

Tax Saver

If you cannot benefit from the full amount of the married couple's allowance because:

- you are not a taxpayer; or
- your tax bill is not big enough,

you can transfer the balance to your spouse or partner by completing form 575(T).

A wife does not need her husband's consent to claim one half of the minimum amount of the married couple's allowance, £1,610 for 2015/16. Alternatively, a married couple can jointly elect for the wife to receive the full minimum amount of the allowance, £3,220 for 2015/16. Such an election:

- must be made using HMRC Form 18;
- must normally be made before the start of the tax year for which it is to apply (except in the year of marriage, when the newly-weds can submit a notice dealing with the reduced married couple's allowance for that year); and
- once made carries on from year to year until changed by the couple.

James Lucas, who is in his mid-80s, had income from pensions of £13,500 in 2015/16. His wife, Mary, who is 25 years younger than James, is still working and earned a salary of £13,250 in 2015/16. She elected to receive one half of the basic married couple's allowance.

James does not pay any tax for 2015/16 as follows:

	£
Pensions	13,500
Less: Personal allowance	10,660
Taxable income	£2,840
Income Tax payable	
£2,840 @ 20 per cent	568.00
Less: Relief for married couple's allowance £8,355 – (1/2 × £3,220) = £6,745 @ 10 per cent but restricted to	568.00

Mary has a tax bill for the year of £369.00 as follows:

	£
Salary	13,250
Less: Personal allowance	10,600
Taxable income	£2,650
Income Tax payable	
£2,650 @ 20 per cent	530.00
Less: Relief for married couple's allowance £1,610 (1/2 × £3,220) @ 10 per cent	161.00
	£369.00

The unused part of James's married couple's allowance amounts to £1,065. By making a claim, this can be transferred to Mary, thereby reducing her tax bill by £106.50 (£1,065 @ 10 per cent) from £369 to £262.50.

Age allowances – income limit

The purpose of the personal age and married couples allowances is to assist elderly taxpayers on low and modest incomes. It follows, therefore, that these allowances are restricted when total income, after permitted reliefs and deductions, exceeds a specified limit – £27,700 for 2015/16. The reduction is £1 for each £2 by which total income is more than the annual stated limit. However:

- the reduced personal allowance cannot come to less than £10,600; and
- there is a minimum amount of £3,220 for the married couple's allowance.

Tax Saver

The personal age allowance decreases first. When it comes to calculating any restriction to the married couple's allowance:

- it is worked out on the income of the husband or the spouse/civil partner with the higher income, as the case may be; and

- it is not affected by the wife's income or that of the other civil partner no matter how much it is.

It follows that any benefit of the higher personal age allowance is lost for a pensioner born before 6 April 1938 when income exceeds £27,820.

The upper income limits beyond which the married couple's allowance reduces to the minimum amount for 2015/16 are:

Claimant's age	Wife's/partner's age (over 74) (£)
born after 5 April 1948	37,970
born between 6 April 1938 and 5 April 1948	37,970
born before 6 April 1938	38,090

An elderly couple, Andrew Dawson, aged 81, and his wife, Monica, aged 79, whose income amounted to £30,000 and £27,750 respectively during 2015/16 paid Income Tax of £3,153.50 and £3,423.00 respectively, worked out as follows:

	Andrew (£)	Monica (£)
Income		
State Pensions	6,029	3,614
Pensions from former employers	20,971	22,936
Building Society Interest	3,000	1,200
	30,000	27,750
Less: Personal allowance	10,600	10,635
Taxable Income	£19,400	£17,115
Income Tax payable		
£19,400/£17,115 @ 20 per cent	3,880.00	3,423.00
Less: Relief for married couple's allowance – £7,265 @ 10 per cent	726.50	
	£3,153.50	£3,423.00

Andrew does not get any benefit from the personal age allowance as his income is more than £27,820. Monica's personal age allowance of £10,660 is reduced by £25 = 0.5 × £50 (£27,750 – income limit of £27,700).

The married couple's allowance of £8,355 is initially restricted by £1,150 = 0.5 × (£30,000 – £27,700). But Andrew's loss of personal allowance of £60 limits the loss of relief to £1,090 (from £8,355 to £7,265).

Blind person's relief

This relief is given to a registered blind person.

Where both:

- husband and wife; or
- civil partners,

are blind, each of them can claim the relief.

If either of them is on a low income and unable to use up his or her relief, any unused part can be transferred to the other even if he or she is not blind.

When a taxpayer first becomes entitled to this special relief, by being registered blind, the relief will also be given for the previous tax year if, at the time, the individual had received the necessary proof of blindness needed to qualify for registration. This concession prevents individuals losing out as a result of any delays in the registration process.

The relief is not available to registered partially-sighted individuals.

Tax credits

03

Tax Saver

If you are on a low or modest income you should be able to claim tax credits. These are:

- Child Tax Credit (CTC), which is paid to individuals who are responsible for children. It does not matter whether claimants do, or do not, work.

- Working Tax Credit (WTC), which is paid to those in work and is targeted at low wage earners and workers who use formal childcare.

Who can claim?

To qualify for tax credits you must be:

- at least 16 years old; and
- physically present in the United Kingdom.

A single joint application must be submitted by:

- married couples;
- couples living together as partners; or
- civil partners.

Both tax credits are dependent on the incomes of the claimants.

Child Tax Credit

CTC is:

- available to individuals responsible for at least one child or qualifying young person; and

- paid by direct transfer to the bank account of the person (usually the mother) mainly responsible for the care of the child or children.

A child is a person under 16 years old or, in the case of a 16-year-old teenager, until 1 September after their 16th birthday.

A qualifying young person is someone who is:

- no longer a child;
- under 20 years old; and
- in full-time education, usually at a school or college; or
- on an approved training course.

You are usually responsible for a child if:

- they live with you permanently;
- you are their main carer and they normally live with you;
- their toys and clothes are kept in your home;
- you feed them and give them spending money.

If you share responsibility for a child and you cannot reach agreement on which of you claim, you can both apply. In this situation the Tax Credit Office will make the decision.

CTC is made up of the following elements:

Rates for 2015/16	Annual (£)	Weekly (£)
Family element	545.00	10.48
Child element (each child)	2,780.00	53.46
Disabled child element*	3,140.00	60.38
Severely disabled child element**	1,275.00	24.51

* in addition to the child element.
** as well as the child and disabled child elements.

Working Tax Credit

To qualify for WTC you must be:

- over 16 years old; or
- aged 25 or over if you are childless or are not disabled.

You have to work a specific number of hours in a week to receive WTC as follows:

Your situation	Working hours a week
Age 25–59	30 hours minimum
Over 60 years old	16 hours minimum
Disabled	16 hours minimum
Single with at least one child	16 hours minimum
Couple with one or more children	Normally at least 24 hours between them – one has to work for at least 16 hours.

There are special rules for some couples:

- with at least one child; and
- who work for less than 24 hours a week between them.

You can claim if you work a minimum of 16 hours a week and:

- you are disabled;
- at least 60 years old; or
- your partner is entitled to Carer's Allowance or is in hospital or prison.

Recipients of WTC may also qualify for assistance with the costs of childcare. To be entitled you must be:

- either a lone working parent;
- a couple both of whom work, with one or both responsible for a child or children; or
- a couple, one of whom works and the other is either incapacitated, a hospital in-patient or in prison.

The childcare element of WTC is paid, with entitlement to WTC, to the person responsible for the care of the child or children. WTC comprises the following elements:

Rates for 2015/16	Annual (£)	Weekly (£)
Basic entitlement	1,960.00	37.69
Additional couples, and lone parent, element	2,010.00	38.65
30-hour element	810.00	15.57
Disability element	2,970.00	57.11
Severe disability element	1,275.00	24.51
Childcare element		
– maximum eligible cost		300.00
– maximum eligible cost for one child		175.00
Percentage of eligible cost covered		70%

Income limits

As an indication, you are probably entitled to tax credits if your annual income is below:

- £26,000 – if you have one child;
- £32,200 – if you have two children;
- £13,100 – if you are single with no children; and
- £18,000 – if you are married or in a couple without children.

How to claim

You have to fill in a form to claim tax credits. A tax credits claim pack can only be obtained from the Tax Credits Helpline.

Claim forms:

- are specific for a tax year; and
- must be signed by the claimant or both parties in the case of a joint claim.

Tax Saver

Do not delay in making your claim since it can only be backdated for a maximum of one month.

Payment

HMRC pay both CTC and WTC to the main carer at either weekly or four-weekly intervals. Where there is a joint claim, the couple can jointly nominate the main carer. If they fail to do so:

- HMRC will make the decision; and
- nominate the main carer, who will usually be the mother or the person receiving Child Benefit.

Tapering

Tax credits are payable in full to a claimant who is receiving:

- income-based Jobseeker's Allowance;
- income support;
- income-related Employment and Support Allowance; or
- State Pension Credit.

Otherwise tax credits taper away at a rate of 41 per cent for each £1 of family income over a threshold of £6,420 (£16,105 where no WTC is claimed). The first £300 of income from pensions, savings and property is excluded. The order of reduction is:

- WTC;
- childcare element of WTC;

- child elements of CTC; and
- family element of CTC.

Tax Saver

For taxpayers claiming tax credits and paying pension contributions, not only will they see their tax bill come down but they may also qualify for an increase in their tax credits award as pension contributions reduce income for tax credit purposes.

Malcolm and Fiona Gifford are married and have three children, one of whom is disabled.

Malcolm works full time, earning £26,200 in 2015/16. Fiona works part time and in the same year earned £7,800 for her 20-hour week.

Their entitlement to tax credits for 2015/16 is £5,498 as follows:

	£	£
WTC		
Basic entitlement	1,960.00	
Additional Couple's element	2,010.00	
30-hour element	810.00	
		4,780.00
CTC		
Child element (3)	8,340.00	
Disabled child element	3,140.00	
Family element	545.00	12,025.00
		16,805.00
Income	34,000.00	
Less: threshold	6,420.00	
	27,580.00	
41 per cent thereof		11,307.00
Total Credits for 2015/16		£5,498.00

Rachel Carson, who looks after her two young sons, is a successful businesswoman on a salary of £45,000 for 2015/16. As Rachel is a single parent she has to pay for childcare and this costs her £280 per week. Her tax credits for 2015/16 work out at £5,260 as follows:

	£	£
WTC		
Basic entitlement	1,960.00	
Lone parent element	2,010.00	
30-hour element	810.00	
Childcare element*	10,192.00	14,972.00
CTC		
Childcare element (2)	5,560.00	
Family element	545.00	6,105.00
		21,077.00
Less: taper 41 per cent × £38,580		15,817.00
(£45,000 – £6,420)		
Total Credits for 2015/16		£5,260.00

* £196 per week being 70 per cent of the cost of £280 per week.

Annual renewal

Every year between April and June time each existing claimant will receive a renewal pack that serves two purposes:

- firstly, to establish actual income for the year just ended and to check on the claimant's circumstances; and
- secondly, to make the claim for the new year.

You have until 31 July in which to complete and return the forms. Once the information you have provided has been processed, you will receive a notice about your final tax credit for the year recently ended.

If you have received too much tax credit you will be expected to refund the excess. This will usually be done by restricting the reward for the year following.

If you have been paid too little tax credit you will receive the extra amount as a single payment.

Changes in circumstances

Once a claimant has been granted tax credits, even for a nil amount, he or she has a duty to advise HMRC within 30 days of certain stipulated changes in circumstances, which are:

- the number of children for which support can be claimed;
- changes in work status;
- not returning to work after leave or a gap;
- marriage, moving in to live with a partner or entering a civil partnership;
- separation or death of a partner;
- going abroad for at least eight weeks;
- leaving the United Kingdom permanently;
- being ill or hospitalized for at least 28 weeks;
- receiving a prison sentence;
- discontinuing payment to a childcare provider;
- a drop of more than £10 a week in the average costs of childcare;
- getting help with the expense of childcare;
- working hours falling below 30 a week (16 if you are claiming childcare costs); and/or
- working hours falling below, or going above, the minimum required to qualify.

You should also notify HMRC as soon as you can of other changes which include:

- the birth of a child;
- you start paying for, or stop getting help with, the costs of childcare;
- you begin claiming benefits or any of your existing benefits change;

- someone in the household becomes disabled; or
- a change to your working hours from under 30 a week to 30 or more.

Income disregard

Not only is a claimant's entitlement to tax credits continuously adjusted by alterations in lifestyle circumstances but it is also affected by changes to income in the award period, namely a tax year.

When a claimant's income drops, a higher award can be immediately requested. However, a drop in income of up to £2,500 in a claim year is disregarded in assessing any increase in entitlement.

Conversely, when income increases the amount of the award will come down. However, a claimant's income for tax credit purposes can increase by as much as £5,000 in a claim year, compared to the previous year, without any reduction in entitlement. This gives more certainty to claimants that their payments will not suddenly be decreased when their income goes up during an award period.

Penalties and interest

The following penalties can be charged:

Offence	Penalty
Failure to notify a change of in-year circumstances or to provide information or evidence required by HMRC	An initial penalty of £300 followed by penalties of up to £60 per day for continuing failure
Over claiming tax credits	Variable depending on mistake or misunderstanding, failure to take reasonable care, serious or deliberate error
Making negligent or fraudulent claims, statements or declarations	Up to £3,000

Interest may be charged by HMRC where tax credits are overpaid, wholly or partly, because of neglect or fraud by a claimant.

Help and advice

If you would like help or advice about tax credits, you can:

- phone the Helpline on 0345 300 3900 (England, Scotland and Wales) or 0345 603 2000 (Northern Ireland);
- go online to **www.gov.uk/taxcredits**; or
- visit a local advice service such as a Citizens' Advice Bureau who may be able to help.

Interest payments and other outgoings

04

The opportunities for claiming tax relief on interest paid on borrowings are few and far between. They are for:

- the purchase, in certain circumstances, of life annuities if you are aged 65 or over;
- buying a share in:
  - an employee-controlled company;
  - a close company (ie controlled by five or fewer shareholders), or lending capital to it;
  - a partnership, or contributing capital to a partnership, if you are a partner;
- buying plant and machinery for use in your job or partnership so long as the plant and machinery attracts capital allowances for tax purposes (see Chapter 7).

Interest is also allowable for tax purposes on a replacement loan where the interest on existing borrowings qualifies for tax relief.

It is important to understand that the purpose for which a loan is advanced governs whether the interest on it will be eligible for tax relief. How the loan is secured is not relevant.

Apart from interest on a loan to acquire buy-to-let property, the interest on which tax relief is due is deducted from your total income in the year of payment. It cannot be spread over the period of accrual, nor can tax relief be claimed if the interest is not actually paid.

> **Tax Saver**
>
> As you do not get tax relief on mortgage interest to buy your own home, it might be worthwhile using any spare cash on deposit with a bank or building society to repay some or all of your mortgage. This is particularly pertinent now, when interest rates on savings are so low.

Home annuity loans

Interest on a loan taken out before 9 March 1999 to purchase an annuity (an investment providing a fixed or increasing annual sum) from an insurance company still attracts tax relief at 23 per cent provided:

- the borrower was at least 65 years old at the time the annuity was purchased;
- not less than 90 per cent of the loan on which the interest is payable went towards buying an annuity for life; or
- security for the loan is the borrower's main residence.

The maximum loan on which tax relief is allowed is £30,000. Where a loan exceeds this limit, tax relief is given on the proportion of the total interest payable equivalent to the £30,000 limit. Income Tax at the special rate of 23 per cent will be deducted at source by the insurance company in working out the regular payments to be made by the borrower.

Buy-to-let property

Interest on a loan taken out to buy, improve or alter a property that you let out is tax deductible. The interest paid each year is set against the rental income from the property and any other properties that you are renting out as part of your income from property business. If the interest paid exceeds the rents less expenses in the same tax year, the excess cannot be set against your other income. The loss can only be carried forward for offset against rental income in future years.

Lionel Foster acquired a buy-to-let flat in 1998 with the assistance of a mortgage of £180,000. His rents less expenses came to £3,600 and £12,700 during 2014/15 and 2015/16 respectively.

	2014/15 (£)	2015/16 (£)
Rents less expenses	3,600	12,700
Less: Loan interest paid	7,200	7,200
Loss carried forward	3,600	3,600
		10,800
2015/16 Net rental income		£1,900

Business loans

Interest on any borrowings by your business can count as a deduction from your business profits for tax purposes. Provided that the borrowed money is issued for business purposes it does not matter whether the interest is paid on:

- a loan taken out for some specific purpose; or
- borrowings because your bank account goes overdrawn.

Interest you pay will also qualify for tax relief where you need to borrow to:

- buy an asset, such as a car or a piece of machinery, for use in your business (the tax allowable interest will be restricted by the extent of any private usage); or
- purchase a share in a partnership of which you are about to become a member, or contribute capital for use in its business.

Perhaps, however, you have business connections with a private company? Interest paid on a loan raised so you can either buy shares in the company, or lend it money for use in its business, is tax deductible. You must either:

- own at least 5 per cent of the company's share capital; or
- hold at least some shares in the company and spend the greater part of your time working in the business.

Employees who need to borrow to buy shares in their company, as part of an employee buy-out, are allowed tax relief on the interest paid on their borrowings.

Gift Aid

Tax Saver

Gift Aid is an Income Tax relief for cash gifts, without limit, by individuals to charities. Under Gift Aid a charity can claim back from HMRC 25p for every £1 you donate.

You can:

- give any amount, large or small, regularly or as a one-off donation; and
- pay by cash, cheque, postal order, standing order, direct debit, or by using your credit or debit card.

For your donation to qualify under Gift Aid you must:

- pay at least as much tax in the tax year in which you make your cash gifts as the charities will reclaim on them; and
- make a declaration to the charity, either orally or in writing, that you want your donation to be regarded as made under Gift Aid.

Tax Saver

If you pay tax at either the 40 per cent or 45 per cent rates, you can claim tax relief on your Gift Aid donations. This is worked out on the difference between the top rate at which you pay and the basic rate of 20 per cent.

Therefore, for every £100 you donate:

Your top rate of tax (%)	Your tax saving (£)	What the charity receives (£)
40	30.00	125.00
45	36.25	125.00

Norman Walton gave donations totalling £2,400 under Gift Aid in 2015/16. Norman is a higher rate taxpayer so he can reduce his tax bill by £600 as follows:

	£
Grossed-up donations – £2,400 × 100 / 80 =	3,000
Tax relief thereon at 40 per cent	1,200
Less: Deducted when making donations	600
Reduction in Income Tax payable	£600

Tax Saver

You can claim to carry back donations so they are treated as if paid in the previous tax year. For example, they can be carried back to 2015/16 so you get the tax relief in that year rather than in 2016/17, provided the donations were:

- made after 5 April 2016; and

- before 31 January 2017 – or the date when you send your 2015/16 Tax Return to your tax office (if earlier).

If you do not pay tax, Gift Aid is not for you.

Gifts of assets to charities

Tax Saver

You can claim relief from both Income Tax and Capital Gains Tax at your top rates of both taxes for the full market value of any gifts of shares, securities or land and buildings to charities at the time of the gift.

The assets that qualify for this type of tax relief are:

- shares or securities listed on a recognized Stock Exchange;
- shares or securities dealt in on any market in the United Kingdom that is designated for this purpose by HMRC;
- units in an authorized unit trust;
- shares in an open-ended investment company;
- an interest in an offshore fund; and
- land and buildings.

Jennifer Pickard pays tax at the higher rate of 40 per cent on a substantial part of her income. In September 2015 she decided to give shares in a quoted company valued at £8,000 to her favourite charity. The taxable capital gain on the shares would have been £3,600 if she had sold them. Jennifer saves tax of £4,208 as follows:

	£
Reduction in Income Tax (40 per cent × £8,000)	3,200
Capital Gains Tax not payable on the gain* (28 per cent × £3,600)	1,008
2015/16 Maximum tax saving	£4,208

* assuming Jennifer had already utilized her Annual Exemption Limit (see Chapter 13).

Payroll giving

If you are in employment there may be another way that you can make tax-efficient gifts to charity. But, first of all, you need to enquire of your employer whether it participates in such an arrangement through a charity arrangement approved by HMRC. If so you can ask your employer to make regular deductions from your salary that, as part of the scheme, will be passed on to the charities of your choice. You will receive full Income Tax relief on such donations. There is no limit to the amount you can contribute this way each year.

Tax Saver

To give £100 costs:

- £80 if you pay tax at the basic rate;
- £60 for a higher rate tax payer; and
- £55 for someone paying tax at the additional rate.

Working in employment

05

Most of us have worked for somebody else at some stage in our lives either on a full-time or part-time basis.

Am I employed?

Generally speaking you are regarded as employed:

- if you work for the same organization from day to day; and
- you do not have the risks associated with the running of a business.

If the answer is 'yes' to most of the following questions then you will correctly have been categorized as having employee status:

- Do you have to do the work yourself?
- Can you be told where to work, when to work, how to work and what to do?
- Can you be moved from job to job?
- Do you have to work a set number of hours?
- Are you paid a regular wage or salary?
- Can you get additional pay for overtime and a bonus?
- Are you entitled to holiday pay and sickness pay when you are away from work unwell?
- Are you responsible for managing anyone else engaged by your employer?

Earnings

The earnings from an employment on which Income Tax is payable are:

- a salary or wage;
- a bonus;

- overtime;
- commission;
- tips or gratuities;
- holiday or sick pay;
- part-time earnings;
- director's salary or fees; and
- benefits-in-kind.

The Pay-As-You-Earn (PAYE) system

The mechanism for collecting the tax due on earnings from an employment is the PAYE system. It is the responsibility of employers to:

- deduct both Income Tax and National Insurance Contributions from the earnings of their employees; and
- pay the total deductions over to HMRC every month.

The PAYE deducted from an employee's earnings is regarded as a credit against the total tax payable by the employee for that tax year. Each employee's individual allowances and reliefs are taken into account by the employer in working out the amount of tax to deduct from the employee's salary or wage. This is possible because HMRC issue all employers with a code number for each employee.

Code numbers

Every employee's annual PAYE Coding Notice sets out:

- on the first lines, the total tax allowances due; and
- on the lines below, the amounts taken away from the allowances.

On the reverse of the form are guidance notes to help you understand how HMRC worked out your tax code.

The PAYE system allows for the net allowances to be spread evenly throughout the tax year in working out the deductions for Income Tax so as to avoid any substantial variation to the amount of the regular salary cheque or pay packet.

All things being equal this system should ensure that the right amount of tax is deducted from your earnings each year. However, it can only work properly and effectively if you promptly tell your tax office of changes in your personal circumstances that affect any of the entries on your Notice of Coding. For example, most Coding Notices for the 2016/17 tax year, beginning on 6 April 2016, were sent out during the early part of the year. This is before your tax office will have received your 2016 Tax Return, stating your income, capital gains, reliefs and allowances for the year to 5 April 2016. It follows, therefore, that the information on which all 2016/17 code numbers have been based is out of date. This is why it is important that you check your code number for 2016/17 and tell your tax office if:

- alterations are required to your allowances of reliefs;
- you have changed jobs or ceased to be employed;
- you have started receiving a pension;
- there has been a big change in your income; or
- you have moved home.

Your tax allowances for 2016/17 should be correct as all the Income Tax allowances for this year were released by the Treasury last November. These are:

	£
Personal	11,000
Transferrable marriage	11,100
Married couples – maximum	8,355
Married couples – minimum	3,220

* from 2016/17 there is only one personal allowance irrespective of a taxpayer's date of birth.

If the 2016 Budget contains any other changes affecting your 2016/17 Coding Notice your tax office will send you details together with an amended Notice.

On page 48 is an illustration of Simon Black's 2016/17 Notice of Coding. Simon is a married man, with two young children, who does not pay tax above the basic rate of 20 per cent. On the first line of the Notice is Simon's personal allowance for 2016/17 of £11,000. The amounts taken away from Simon's allowances are on the lines below. These are as follows:

- The first three deductions are the taxable figures of the benefits-in-kind of a company car, free fuel for private motoring and private medical insurance cover provided to Simon and his family by his employer. The Income Tax payable by Simon on these benefits is, therefore, collected by restricting his allowances by the taxable amount of the benefits.

- The last deduction is for tax of £84.00 underpaid in 2014/15. For a number of reasons the allowances given, or deductions included, in Simon's Notice of Coding may turn out not to be always totally correct. If, as a result, tax is underpaid, this is usually collected in a subsequent year by restricting allowances in the coding. In the illustration a restriction of Simon's 2016/17 allowances by £420 will enable HMRC to collect the underpayment of £84.00 (£420 @ 20 per cent) from him.

The combined effect of these adjustments is to leave Simon with allowances of just £2,281 to be set against his salary for 2016/17. His code number is 228L. It is not difficult to see that there is a direct link between Simon's allowances and his code number. The suffix letter added to the coding is a way of identifying the category into which a taxpayer falls:

- L is for a code with the basic personal allowance.
- M shows that you have received 10 per cent of your spouse's/ partner's personal allowance.
- N tells you that you have transferred 10 per cent of your personal allowance.
- OT means that:
  - your personal allowance has been used up;
  - you have started a new job and do not have a form P45; or
  - you fail to provide your new employer with the information needed to give you a tax code.
- T applies in many other cases, for example:
  - if you ask your tax office not to use any of the letters listed above; or
  - if there are items in the coding which need to be reviewed.

There are also a number of other codes:

- BR: this tells your employer to deduct tax at the basic rate.
- NT: no tax will be deducted.
- DO: tax will be deducted at the higher rate of 40 per cent.
- DI: tax will be taken off at the additional rate of 45 per cent.

- Prefix K: a K code is given to employees whose total deductions including taxable benefits exceed their personal allowances. The amount of the negative allowances is then added to the pay on which tax is payable. The system of K codes ensures that taxpayers pay all the tax due on their excess benefits evenly throughout the tax year under the PAYE system.

FIGURE 5.1

HM Revenue
& Customs

MR S BLACK
12 CHURCH RISE
BROADWOOD
PT3 8ZL

    35800

Dear MR S BLACK

National Insurance number   BZ 62 24 17 A

This is to tell you your tax code(s) for the year 6 April 2016 to 5 April 2017

Your tax code is used by your employer(s) and/or pension provider(s) to work out how much Income Tax to collect from your pay or pension. We send them a separate tax code notice.

This is how we worked out your tax code(s)

Your tax-free amount		For help
Personal Allowance	£11,000	Go to note 1
Total	£11,000	
Less Car Benefit	£3,400	Go to note 2
Less Car Fuel Benefit	£4,199	Go to note 3
Less Medical Insurance	£700	Go to note 4
Less Unpaid Tax	£420	Go to note 5
Total tax-free amount	£2,281	

Your total tax-free amount is used as follows	Tax code	For help
BROADWOOD ENGINEERS LTD £2,281 of this income is tax-free	228 L	Go to note 6
This totals your tax-free amount £2,281		Go to note 7

How tax is worked out using your tax code

The coding notice issued to Simon Black for 2016/17 tells him that his tax-free amount for the year is £2,281. He earns £34,320 per annum in his job.

The deduction for tax is worked out as follows:

	£
Pay from employment	34,320.00
Less: tax-free amount for year	2,280.00
Tax due on	32,040.00
Income Tax payable £32,000 @ 20 per cent	6,400.00
£40 @ 40 per cent	16.00
	£6,416.00

To work out the weekly amounts of pay and tax, divide the pay and tax payable for the year by 52:

Weekly pay is £34,320 ÷ 52 = £660.00

Weekly tax is £6,416 ÷ 52 = £123.38

To work out the equivalent monthly amount divide by 12:

Monthly pay is £34,320 ÷ 12 = £2,860.00

Monthly tax is £6,416 ÷ 12 = £534.66

Form P60

Shortly after the end of each tax year every employer sends HMRC a Return summarizing:

- the names of all employees;
- their earnings during that tax year; and
- the deductions made for both Income Tax and National Insurance Contributions.

FIGURE 5.2

P60 End of Year Certificate

Tax year to 5 April 2016

To the employee:

Please keep this certificate in a safe place as **you will need it if you have to fill in a tax return. You also need it to make a claim for tax credits or to renew your claim.**

It also helps you check that your employer is using the correct National Insurance number and deducting the right rate of National Insurance contributions.

By law you are required to tell HM Revenue & Customs about any income that is not fully taxed, even if you are not sent a tax return.

HM Revenue & Customs

The figures marked ★ should be used for your tax return, if you get one

Employee's details

Surname	BLACK
Forenames or initials	SIMON

National Insurance number: BZ 62 24 17 A

Works/payroll number:

Pay and Income Tax details

	Pay £ p	Tax deducted £ p
In previous employment(s)		
In this employment ★	34,320 00	6,751 00
Total for year	34,320 00	6,751 00

if refund mark 'R'

Final tax code: 155 L

National Insurance contributions in this employment

NIC table letter	Earnings at the Lower Earnings Limit (LEL) (where earnings are equal to or exceed the LEL) £	Earnings above the LEL, up to and including the Primary Threshold (PT) £	Earnings above the PT, up to and including the Upper Accrual Point (UAP) £	Earnings above the UAP, up to and including the Upper Earnings Limit (UEL) £	Employee's contributions due on all earnings above the PT £ p
A	5,824	2,236	26,260		

Statutory payments included in the pay In this employment figure above

	£ p		£ p		£ p
Statutory Maternity Pay		Statutory Paternity Pay		Additional Statutory Paternity Pay/ Shared Parental Pay	
Statutory Adoption Pay					

Other details

Student Loan deductions in this employment (whole £s only)   £

To employee

SIMON BLACK
12 CHURCH RISE
BROADWOOD
PT3 8ZL

Your employer's full name and address (including postcode)

BROAD WOOD ENGINEERS LTD
BRIDCE STREET
BROADWOOD
PT3 7GN

Employer PAYE reference: 28/B604

Certificate by Employer/Paying Office:
This form shows your total pay for Income Tax purposes in this employment for the year.
Any overtime, bonus, commission etc, Statutory Sick Pay, Statutory Maternity Pay, Statutory Paternity Pay, Additional Statutory Paternity Pay/Shared Parental Pay or Statutory Adoption Pay is included.

P60(Single sheet)(2015-16)   Do not destroy   xxxxxxxx   HMRC 12/14

By 31 May following the end of a tax year, your employer must give you your Form P60 on paper or electronically. This is a certificate of your earnings for the past tax year. It also shows:

- how much Income Tax and National Insurance Contributions you paid;
- the Code Number used in working out the deductions for Income Tax;
- your NINO;
- your employer's name and address.

On page 50 there is an illustration of the Form P60 sent to Simon Black by his employer for 2015/16. This shows:

- the tax deducted from his earnings of £34,320 in the year amounted to £6,751, based on a tax code of 155L;
- he made National Insurance Contributions totalling £3,151.20.

Starting work

Your employer will ask you to fill in HMRC's new starter checklist if you:

- are starting a job for the first time;
- have not already been in work during the tax year;
- are also in another job; or
- receive the State or an occupational pension.

The information on the new starter checklist enables your employer to:

- work out your tax code;
- set you up on their payroll software; and
- register you with HMRC.

As a result the right deductions for Income Tax and National Insurance can be made from your wage or salary.

Moving jobs

Whenever you change your job your old employer will give you Parts 1A, 2 and 3 of Form P45. On this form are:

- your name and address;
- the name and address of your past employer;
- your tax district and reference number;
- your code number at the date of leaving;
- your accumulative salary and the tax deductions for the tax year up to the date that you leave; and
- your salary and tax deductions from the last employment unless this information is the same as the accumulative figures.

Your ex-employer submits the first part of the Form P45 to their tax district online.

Parts 2 and 3 of the Form P45 must be given:

- to your new employer; or
- Jobcentre Plus if you are not in work.

Your new employer will enter your address and the date you start your new job before sending Part 3 of the form to their own tax office. The information on the form allows your current employer to make the correct deductions for Income Tax and National Insurance from your salary or wage from the date you start your new job.

You should keep Part 1A of the form for your own records because it may be helpful when you come to prepare your own tax return.

Tax-deductible expenses

The rules allowing you to claim tax relief on expenses connected with your employment are extremely restricted. You are denied tax relief on almost all types of expense that are not ultimately borne by your employer. This is because, as an employee, you have to show that any expenditure is incurred 'wholly, exclusively and necessarily' in performing the duties of your employment. If your employer will not foot the bill for the expenditure involved, then HMRC take the view that it was incurred as a matter of choice rather than of necessity. Nevertheless, some business expenses paid personally are deductible from your income and should be claimed on your Tax Return.

Tax Saver

Tax-deductible expenses include:

- Annual subscriptions to a professional body.
- Business use of your own car and telephone.
- Travel and overnight expenses.
- Clothing and upkeep of tools – HMRC and the trade unions have agreed flat-rate allowances for the upkeep of tools and special clothing in most classes of industry. The current rates are set out in Appendix 2. As an alternative you can claim a deduction for the actual amounts spent on these items.
- Payment by directors or employees for work-related insurance cover. Tax relief is also allowed on meeting the cost of uninsured liabilities.

Tax-free expenses

Tax Saver

The cost of most expenses you incur in your work is ultimately met by your employer, who either reimburses you on an expense claim or pays for them direct. Tax free for everyone are:

- Free or subsidized meals in a staff canteen, providing the facilities can be used by all staff.
- Sporting and recreational facilities.
- Staff parties, providing the annual cost to the employer is no more than £150 per head.
- Awards for long service of at least 20 years. The cost of the articles purchased by the employer must not exceed £50 for each year of service.
- Gifts not exceeding £250 in the tax year to an employee from a third party by reason of his or her employment.
- One routine health check and one medical screening each year.
- Eye tests and corrective glasses if your employer is required, by law, to provide eye and eyesight tests for you because of the work you do.
- Up to £500 each year for recommended medical treatment.

- Work-related training expenses including fees, travel, reasonable subsistence and the cost of any books.
- The cost of out-placement counselling and retraining courses for both full- and part-time employees.
- Equipment or facilities provided to disabled people to enable them to carry out their jobs.
- Computer equipment loaned to employees before 6 April 2006 providing the cash equivalent of the benefit does not come to more than £500 annually. Any excess over £500 is taxable.
- One mobile telephone per employee for private use. But the exemption continues for multiple telephones provided to employees before 6 April 2006.
- Childcare facilities at the workplace or elsewhere (but not on domestic premises).
- Employer-supported childcare of up to £55 a week. For higher and additional rate taxpayers joining an employer's scheme after 5 April 2011 the relief is limited to £28 and £25 respectively. Employers can either contract with an approved child carer or provide childcare vouchers.
- Up to £4 per week paid to you by your employer for working at home as part of your employment contract. You are not required to produce any supporting evidence of the costs you incur.
- Accommodation and subsistence expenses when your duties require you to travel abroad. HMRC have published a list of benchmarks for use by your employer. Only payments in excess of the rates are taxable.
- Personal incidental expenses when you stay away from home overnight on business. The most common expenses covered are newspapers, telephone calls to home and laundry. The tax-free limits, including VAT, are £5 per night for stays anywhere in the United Kingdom and £10 per night elsewhere. Where these limits are exceeded the whole payment becomes payable – not the excess.
- Bicycle and cycling safety equipment made available to employees mainly to get them between home and work.
- Parking facilities for cars, motorcycles or bicycles at or near your place of work.
- A work bus service.
- The cost of infrequent private transport when you have been working late and either public transport is no longer available or it would be unreasonable to expect you to use it at a late hour. Infrequent late working means working until at least 9.00 pm not more than 60 times in a tax year.

- Mileage allowances where employees use their car, van, motorcycle or pedal cycle on business.

The tax-free rates laid down by HMRC for 2015/16 are:

Cars and vans	
– First 10,000 miles	45p per mile
– Excess	25p per mile
Motorcycles	24p per mile
Bicycles	20p per mile

Tax Saver

Employees are taxed on payments made by their employers over and above the rates in the table, but they can claim back and get tax relief on the difference where their employers pay them less than the permitted rate.

Employee travel

The cost of travelling between home and work is not allowable for tax purposes, other than for disabled employees who are given financial help by their employers with home-to-work travel on public transport or by some other means.

However, tax relief is allowed on all your business travel where your journey starts from either home or your permanent workplace. Where the full cost of a journey is not reimbursed by your employer, you can claim tax relief on the excess miles not paid for by your employer.

(a) Site-based workers

These are employees who work at a number of different places for periods of a few weeks or months at a time. Travelling expenses reimbursed to them are tax free providing:

- the worker initially expects the posting not to exceed two years, and the stay actually does last for less than this time;

- there is no requirement for an employee to return to his or her permanent workplace when each site job comes to an end; and
- an employee's work on-site may be considered as a single continuous period even if he or she is occasionally moved off-site.

(b) Employees with areas

The geographical area covered by employees such as salesmen is treated as their permanent place of work. The following special rules apply:

- All travel within the area is eligible for tax relief.
- Where an employee lives outside his or her area, travel to the start of the area is classified as home-to-work travel and is taxable if paid for by the employer.
- The entire country is likely to be the area for any employee whose duties extend to servicing customers throughout the whole of the United Kingdom.

All travelling appointments of service engineers are treated as business travel qualifying for tax relief.

(c) More than one workplace

No tax relief is due for travel from home to either place of work for employees with more than one permanent place of location. It is HMRC's view that a workplace is likely to be considered as permanent if:

- an employee regularly performs 40 per cent or more of the duties of the employment there;
- customers, suppliers and others would expect to make contact with the employee there;
- the employee has an office or desk and support services.

Home working

A growing number of people are now giving up the daily commute in favour of working from home, on either a full-time or a part-time basis. This is being made increasingly possible because of modern technology.

However, to get tax benefits, you must be able to demonstrate that you work from home as a necessity rather than by choice. If you satisfy this test you should be able to claim tax relief on:

- a proportion of your household costs such as heating, lighting, telephone and water (if any);

- use of your car, computer and tools for your employer's business; and

- other expenses you incur on stationery, books and professional subscriptions for the business.

Benefits-in-kind

Employees (including full-time working directors who own 5 per cent or under of the company's shares) earning less than £8,500 per annum, including expenses, are not taxed on most benefits or perks provided by their employers. In addition to the list of tax-free expenses, the most valuable non-taxable benefits for this class of employee are private medical insurance and a company car.

Other directors and employees (including full-time working directors), whose total earnings, including expenses, exceed £8,500 per annum, are generally taxed on the actual value of any employment-related benefits and taxable expenses. Information about your expense payments and benefits-in-kind is supplied by your employer to your tax office each year on Form P11D. Your employer should give you a copy of this form by 6 July following the end of the tax year. It sets out your employer's calculations of your taxable payments and cash equivalents of benefits-in-kind. It is up to you to claim those that are not taxable. This should not cause you any problem where expenses such as travelling and entertaining have genuinely arisen from the performance of the duties of your employment.

There are set rules for calculating some benefits.

(a) Company cars

The tax charge is based on a percentage of the list price of a car (including qualifying accessories) but graduated according to the level of the car's carbon dioxide (CO_2) emissions. The minimum charge is 5 per cent of list price, increasing to a maximum of 37 per cent if CO_2 emissions are above the prescribed level.

In view of their higher emissions of pollutants diesel cars are subject to a 3 per cent supplementary charge. However, even for diesel cars the maximum charge cannot exceed 37 per cent of a car's price.

The car benefit charges for cars with an approved CO_2 emissions figure for the 2015/16 tax year are as follows:

CO_2 emissions in g/km	% of list price that is taxed	
	Petrol	Diesel
0–50	5	8
51–75	9	11
76–94	13	16
95	14	17
100	15	18

CO_2 emissions in g/km	% of list price that is taxed	
	Petrol	Diesel
105	16	19
110	17	20
115	18	21
120	19	22
125	20	23
130	21	24
135	22	25
140	23	26
145	24	27
150	25	28
155	26	29
160	27	30
165	28	31
170	29	32
175	30	33
180	31	34
185	32	35
190	33	36
195	34	37
200	35	37
205	36	37
210	37	37

Where the CO_2 figure for a car is not a multiple of 5, it is rounded down to the nearest 5.

The regime extends to all cars, not just new ones. However, special rules apply to:

- older cars (those registered before 1 January 1998); and
- cars first registered on or after 1 January 1998 with no CO_2 emissions.

Cars first registered before 1 January 1998 will have no CO_2 emissions figures and, therefore, the taxable car benefit is worked out on a percentage of list price based on engine size:

Engine size (cc)	% of list price which is taxed
Up to 1,400	15
1,401–2,000	22
2,001 or more	32

The same applies to cars registered on or after 1 January 1998 with no CO_2 emissions figures, as follows:

Engine size (cc)	% of list price that is taxed
Up to 1,400	15 (18 per cent if diesel)
1,401–2,000	25 (28 per cent if diesel)
2,001 or more	37
No cylinder capacity	37

Mileage between home and work counts as private, not business, usage except in a car made available to an employee who:

- has a travelling appointment;
- travels from home to a temporary place of work if the distance travelled is less than the distance between the normal place of work and the temporary place of work; or
- is a home worker and travels from home to another place of work in the performance of his or her duties.

There are several other circumstances where home-to-work travel in an employer-provided car is considered to be private use but is disregarded for tax purposes. These are where the car is provided:

- to a disabled person for home-to-work travel and there is no other private use;
- for home-to-work travel when public transport is disrupted; and
- for late-night journeys home from work.

(b) Fuel benefits

If your employer pays for fuel for your private motoring, this also gives rise to a taxable benefit on which you have to pay Income Tax. The taxable amount is calculated on the car benefit percentage for the CO_2 emissions of your car multiplied by 22,100, giving the following taxable benefits for the 2015/16 tax year:

CO₂ emissions in g/km	% of £22,100 that is taxed		Taxable benefit (£)	
	Petrol	Diesel	Petrol	Diesel
0–50	5	8	1,105	1,768
51–75	9	11	1,989	2,652
76–94	13	16	2,873	3,536
95	14	17	3,094	3,757
100	15	18	3,315	3,978
105	16	19	3,536	4,199
110	17	20	3,757	4,420
115	18	21	3,978	4,641
120	19	22	4,199	4,862
125	20	23	4,420	5,083
130	21	24	4,641	5,304
135	22	25	4,862	5,525
140	23	26	5,083	5,746
145	24	27	5,304	5,967
150	25	28	5,525	6,188
155	26	29	5,746	6,409
160	27	30	5,967	6,630
165	28	31	6,188	6,851
170	29	32	6,409	7,072
175	30	33	6,630	7,293
180	31	34	6,851	7,514
185	32	35	7,072	7,735
190	33	36	7,293	7,956
195	34	37	7,514	8,177
200	35	37	7,735	8,177
205	36	37	7,956	8,177
210	37	37	8,177	8,177

The benefit is:

- reduced to zero if the full cost of fuel for all your private motoring is reimbursed to your employer;
- proportionately reduced if you stop enjoying the use of free fuel for non-business motoring part way through a tax year; and
- not charged for any period of at least 30 days during which your car cannot be used or is unavailable to you.

Tax Saver

You will often be better off paying for your own fuel for non-business mileage.

(c) Company vans

If your employer provides you with a company van without any unrestricted use, no matter the age or size of the van, you are taxed on a fixed amount of £3,150.

The benefit on a company van with zero emissions is 20 per cent of the fixed van benefit charge. This is equivalent to a taxable benefit of £630 in 2015/16.

There is an additional benefit of £594 where your employer pays for fuel for private mileage.

(d) Pooled vehicles

The private use of a car from an employer's pool of vehicles will not give rise to a tax charge on an employee provided:

- any home-to-work travel is merely incidental to business use; and
- the vehicle is not garaged at or near the employee's home overnight.

(e) Living accommodation

In some trades it is established practice for an employer to provide living accommodation. This can also be desirable where there is a security risk. No Income Tax liability arises in either set of circumstances.

In other situations Income Tax is chargeable on the annual value of the property after deducting any rent paid for it. For these purposes the annual valuation is broadly equivalent to the gross rateable value. Estimated rateable values will be used for new properties not appearing on the domestic rating list.

An additional tax charge arises where the accommodation costs more than £75,000. This is worked out by applying HMRC's official interest rate (see below) to the excess of the cost price above £75,000.

(f) Beneficial loans

The rules dealing with interest-free or low-rate-interest loans from an employer are as follows:

- The taxable benefit is worked out by applying HMRC's official rate of interest to the loan, currently 3 per cent.
- Any interest actually paid on the loan reduces the amount of the benefit.
- No tax charge arises where all of an employee's cheap or interest-free loans, excluding loans that qualify for tax relief, total less than £10,000.
- There is no tax charge where the loan is for a purpose on which the interest would qualify for tax relief (see Chapter 4).

(g) Medical insurance

You will be taxed on the cost of private medical insurance premiums paid by your employer for you or other members of your family. Not subject to tax is the cost of medical insurance cover, or actual medical treatment overseas, while away on business.

(h) Relocation expenses

An employee who changes job, or is relocated by his or her employer, is not taxed on the costs of a relocation package up to £8,000. This limit applies to each job-related move. There are specific definitions for the removal expenses and benefits that qualify for exemption within the monetary limit.

Employee share ownership

(a) Under a Share Incentive Plan

- Employers can give employees up to £3,600 of shares free of Income Tax and National Insurance.
- Some or all of these shares can be awarded to employees for reaching performance targets.
- Employees are able to buy partnership shares out of their pre-tax salary or wage up to a maximum of 10 per cent of salary or £1,800 a year, free of Income Tax and National Insurance.
- Employers can match partnership shares by giving employees up to two free shares for each partnership share they buy.
- Employees who sell their shares are liable to Capital Gains Tax only on any increase in the value of their shares after they come out of a plan.
- Free and matching shares must normally be kept in the plan for at least three years – employees can take partnership shares out of the plan at any time.
- Shares must come out of the plan when employees leave and some employees may lose their free and matching shares if they leave their jobs within three years of getting the shares.
- Dividends, up to £1,500 annually, paid on the shares are tax free providing they are reinvested in additional shares in the company and retained for at least three years.
- Employees who keep their shares in a plan for five years pay no Income Tax or National Insurance on those shares.

- Employees who take their shares out of a plan after three years pay Income Tax and National Insurance on no more than the initial value of the shares – any increase in the value of their shares while in the plan is free of Income Tax and National Insurance.
- Capital Gains Tax roll-over relief is available for existing shareholders of smaller companies who want to sell their shares to a new plan trust to be used for the benefit of employees.

(b) The main features of a Savings-Related Share Option Scheme

- It operates in combination with either a bank or building society SAYE savings contract under which employees save a fixed regular amount each month.
- The maximum amount that can be saved is £500 per month over either a three- or five-year period.
- The price at which options can be offered to directors and employees cannot be less than 80 per cent of the market value of the shares at the time the options are granted.
- The receipt of the options and any increase in the value of the shares between the time that the options are granted and the date when they are exercised are free of Income Tax.

(c) Under an Approved Profit-Sharing Scheme

- A company makes an allocation of profits to trustees who, in turn, use the contribution in acquiring shares in the company that are subsequently allotted to employees.
- The limit on the market value of shares that may be appropriated to any one individual in each tax year is 10 per cent of salary, with a minimum limit of £3,000 and a maximum of £8,000.
- There is no Income Tax liability when the shares are set aside or if they are retained by the trustees of the scheme for three years.

(d) Inland Revenue Approved Share Option Plan

- No liability to Income Tax is imposed on a director or employee who acquires, or disposes of, ordinary shares under such a plan.

- The market value of shares, at the time of the grant of the option, over which an individual holds unexercised rights under the plan must not exceed £30,000.

- An option must be exercised not less than three, or more than 10, years after it is granted, or under three years after a previous exercise.

- The gain is measured by the difference between the sale proceeds and the cost of acquiring the shares, and is charged to Capital Gains Tax at the time of disposal.

- The price payable must be fixed at the time of the grant and must not be less than the market value of the shares at that date.

(e) Employee shareholder shares

- Employee shareholders are either issued or allotted shares worth a minimum of £2,000 in consideration of an employee shareholder agreement.

- For Income Tax purposes employee shareholders will be deemed to have paid £2,000 for their shares, thereby reducing the tax charge at the time of issue or allotment.

- These shares are exempt from Capital Gains Tax when they are disposed of.

Enterprise Management Incentives

Enterprise Management Incentives are aimed at:

- helping small companies attract and retain the key people they need; and

- rewarding employees for taking a risk by investing their time and skills in helping small companies achieve their potential.

Normally, without any charge to Income Tax or National Insurance, companies can grant share options to employees worth up to £250,000 at the time of the grant.

A qualifying employee is one who must spend at least 25 hours a week, or if less, 75 per cent of his or her working time on the business of that company.

Payments on termination of employment

It is often the practice for an employee to be paid a lump sum on the termination of an employment. If the right to receive the lump sum arose during the employment then it is taxable in full in the same way as any other earnings. Otherwise the lump sum payment is either wholly or partly tax free. Such payments are free of tax where:

- the employment ceases because of the accidental death, injury or disability of the employee; or

- most of the employee's time was spent working overseas for the employer.

Where the lump sum payment is made at a time other than on death or retirement, then the first £30,000 is tax free. It is only the excess of any payment over £30,000 that is taxable.

Any statutory redundancy repayment you receive, although it is itself exempt from tax, has to be added to any other lump sum payment from your employer in working out the Income Tax due on the amount.

It is not unusual for redundancy and employment termination settlements to provide for benefits, such as membership of a company medical insurance scheme, to continue after the employment has come to an end. Such payments and benefits are taxed only to the extent that they actually arise, and in the year in which they are received or enjoyed.

Belinda Morrison was made redundant in May 2015. Under her employment termination settlement she received lump sum payments of £17,000 and £20,000 on 22 May 2015 and 8 April 2016 respectively. She was also permitted to retain her membership of her employer's company medical insurance scheme for four years at an annual cost to her employer of £1,000. Belinda's total redundancy package for 2015/16 comes to £27,000. As this is below the £30,000 exemption limit she does not pay tax on any part of the package she received in 2015/16. The balance of the exemption limit of £3,000 is carried forward to 2016/17 to be set against the cash payment of £20,000 and the medical insurance benefit of £1,000. For 2016/17, therefore, Belinda's old employer will deduct tax on £18,000.

Value Added Tax 06

Value Added Tax (VAT) is a system for taxing what people spend. It is also administered by HMRC. The National Advice Service (NAS) is the main contact point for businesses. The NAS telephone number is 0300 200 3700.

What is VAT?

VAT is a self-assessed tax charged on:

- the supply of goods and services in the United Kingdom; and
- the import of goods and certain services into the United Kingdom.

It applies where a taxable person in business makes supplies that are taxable supplies.

Rates of VAT

There are three rates of VAT: a standard rate of 20 per cent, a reduced rate of 5 per cent and a zero rate. Most of the goods and services supplied in the United Kingdom are liable to tax at the standard rate. Among the goods and services liable at the two lower rates are:

- Supplies charged at 5 per cent:
  - domestic fuel and power;
  - renovations and alterations of dwellings; and
  - residential conversions.
- Zero-rated supplies:
  - food sold in shops;
  - books, magazines and newspapers;

- babywear;
- children's clothing and footwear;
- construction of new homes; and
- passenger transport.

Exempt supplies

Some goods and services have no VAT on them. These include:

- education and training;
- health and welfare;
- insurance;
- land; and
- finance services and banking.

If you sell goods or supply services that are exempt:

- you do not charge VAT on your income; and
- you cannot recover VAT incurred on the purchases and expenses of your business.

Special rules apply where your business makes both chargeable and exempt supplies.

Registration

If you are just starting up a business it is unlikely you will need to register for VAT immediately. Only when the value of your taxable supplies reaches £82,000 in a 'rolling' 12-month period is it compulsory to apply for registration. In working out the turnover of your business for this purpose, remember that taxable supplies are not just those liable at the standard rate but include supplies liable to tax at the lower rates of 5 per cent and zero.

Simon Potter started up in business in August 2014. He has been successful in building up his turnover each month. Looking back from the end of January 2016, his turnover for the previous 12 months was £76,000. But when he did the same exercise a month later this figure had increased to £83,000. Simon had to notify liability to register by 31 March 2016 and was registered for VAT from 1 April 2016.

You also need to register if the taxable supplies of your business in the next 30 days above are likely to exceed the registration limit of £82,000. Also, do not delay making an application for registration if you acquire an existing business where the previous owner was VAT registered. Sometimes it is possible for you to take on the same registration number as that of the previous owner.

You can only avoid registration if you can satisfy HMRC that either:

- your taxable turnover is expected to decline so that, from then on, it will remain at an annual level under £80,000; or
- your business activities are such that, if registration was in place, you would normally receive repayments of VAT.

You can apply for VAT registration by either:

- using HMRC's online services; or
- downloading Form VAT1 and sending the completed form in the post.

Applying online:

- is easier, faster and more secure;
- is certain as you get an immediate acknowledgement that your application has been received by HMRC; and
- allows you to access your certificate of registration through 'Your HMRC services' page.

You should find the VAT notices and leaflets published by HMRC useful in helping you to understand and deal with VAT aspects of your business. Some of these, available from the NAS, are listed in Appendix 3 on page 263.

Voluntary registration

Sometimes there are benefits from VAT registration even though the turnover of your business is below the compulsory limit for registration. Voluntary registration is allowed providing you can show that you are, or will be, making some taxable supplies.

> ### Tax Saver
>
> An advantage of voluntary registration is that you can reduce your costs by recovering VAT incurred on your business expenses, including VAT paid on certain start-up costs and on the acquisition of assets such as computers and printers.

Voluntary registration is also beneficial where:

- customers will only deal with a supplier who is registered for VAT; or
- the image of your business will be enhanced.

But if your customers are the general public, voluntary registration is unlikely to be to your advantage. They cannot recover the VAT charged on your goods and services so you may be putting yourself at a price dis-advantage compared to your competitors.

Cancellation of registration

You can apply to HMRC to deregister your business from VAT:

- where the taxable turnover in the previous year was below the registration threshold of £82,000; or
- the anticipated turnover in the coming 12 months will be below £80,000.

Deregistration is compulsory where:

- you cease to trade; or
- you sell your business.

Help from HMRC

Telephone support is available on the VAT, Customs and Excise Helpline at 0300 200 3700. If you want to know more about VAT educational oppor-tunities you can call the Customer Service Team on 0300 123 1083.

VAT invoices

There are a number of items that you must show on all VAT invoices issued by your business. These mandatory requirements are:

- the date of issue;
- a sequential number that uniquely identifies the invoice;
- your VAT identification number;
- the full name and address of both your own business and that of your customer;
- a description of the quantity and nature of the goods supplied or services rendered;
- the time of the supply;
- the net unit price;
- the gross amount payable, excluding VAT;
- the rate of VAT charged; and
- the amount of VAT payable.

There are also other specific requirements but these only apply in certain circumstances such as supplies to and from other EU countries.

You are also allowed to issue invoices electronically. Furthermore you can agree with your customers that they will raise the invoices for the goods or services you have supplied to them. This practice is known as self-billing.

Records, accounting and returns

If your business is VAT registered you must:

- render tax invoices for all taxable supplies of goods and services;
- retain copies of all VAT invoices issued and received, filed in an orderly manner;
- keep proper business and accounting records;
- maintain an account showing the calculations of your VAT liability for each VAT period; and
- make timely VAT Returns to HMRC.

The VAT payable, or repayable, each period is the simple difference between your VAT output tax and input tax. Output tax is what you charge on the goods and services (outputs) to your customers. Input tax is what you incur on the purchases and expenses (inputs) of running your business.

Totalling the VAT on your outputs and inputs each month should make it fairly straightforward to bring together the information you need to complete the VAT Return – Form VAT100 – for the accounting periods shown on your registration certificate.

Beth Way runs a hairdressing salon which is VAT registered. She has been given quarterly VAT accounting periods in line with the calendar quarters. She accounts for VAT as a retailer on the basis of the income received each quarter. Her VAT account for the three months to the end of March 2016 was:

	£	£
Output Tax		
January	1,940	
February	1,830	
March	2,070	
Total	5,840	5,840
Input Tax		
January	220	
February	160	
March	250	
Total	630	630
Net amount due to HMRC		**£5,210**

The various boxes on your VAT Return can be filled in from the figures in your VAT account and the tax-exclusive values of your outputs and inputs for the period.

Make sure you submit each Return and pay what is due to HMRC within the stipulated time limit. If the VAT you have reclaimed on the purchases and expenses of the business exceeds the VAT on your turnover for the period, the Return will show you are entitled to a repayment, which will be sent direct to your bank account.

If you wish, you can request that your quarterly VAT Return periods coincide with your financial year.

Online filing of Returns

All businesses, irrespective of their turnover, must:

- file VAT returns online; and
- pay any VAT due electronically.

There are a number of benefits from online filing such as up to an extra seven days to:

- file your return; and
- pay any VAT due.

To pay by Direct Debit, the internet, telephone or BACS Direct Payment you need the following information:

Sort code: 08-32-00   Account number: 11963155
Account Name: HMRC VAT

Quote your VAT registration number leaving no gaps.

When signing up for online filing you should have:

- provided an e-mail address; and
- set up an e-mail reminder. This will be the only communication to you from HMRC that it is now time to complete a Return.

Input tax

The actual amount of input tax on purchases does not matter quite so much when the Flat Rate Scheme is used; see page 79. For other businesses it is only the input tax on the costs of the business that can be claimed when VAT Returns are completed. Sometimes expenses may be incurred where input tax cannot be claimed at all. Examples are:

- business entertaining; and
- private purchases paid for through your business.

Occasionally there may be a need to apportion input tax, such as that on home telephone bills incurred partly for business and partly for private purposes. Apportionment is best done on a percentage basis which, provided it is reasonable, HMRC can be expected to accept.

Motor cars and fuel

Businesses directly concerned with motoring, such as new car dealers, vehicle hirers, taxi drivers or driving schools, may be able to reclaim all input tax on cars that they buy or lease. Input tax cannot be claimed back on cars bought by other businesses and made available for private use. However, it may be possible to claim 50 per cent of the input tax on the rental payments where cars are leased.

There are two alternative methods for dealing with input tax on motor fuel, namely:

- all input tax is claimed and a fixed-scale charge to take account of private use is applied. From 1 May 2015 the fuel scale charges, based on a 20 per cent rate, for a three-month period are as follows:

CO_2 emissions in g/km	Scale charge (£)	VAT due (£)
124 and below	133	22.16
125–129	200	33.33
130–134	213	35.50
135–139	227	37.83
140–144	240	40.00
145–149	254	42.33

CO_2 emissions in g/km	Scale charge (£)	VAT due (£)
150–154	267	44.50
155–159	281	46.83
160–164	294	49.00
165–169	308	51.33
170–174	320	53.33
175–179	334	55.66
180–184	347	57.83
185–189	361	60.16
190–194	374	62.33
195–199	388	64.66
200–204	401	66.83
205–209	415	69.16
210–214	428	71.33
215–219	441	73.50
220–224	455	75.83
225 and above	468	78.00

- no input tax is claimed and the fixed-scale charge is ignored. If you intend to deal with motor fuel this way you should write to HMRC to tell them.

Input tax on repairs and maintenance of business cars can be claimed whichever way you decide to deal with motor fuel.

Bad debts

Late or non-payment of bills can often have a serious impact on both the cash flow and profitability of a business. When it comes to bad debts it is only when a debt is more than six months old that an adjustment can be made to recover VAT accounted for on that debt in a previous VAT Return.

Adjustments for bad debts, although not separately shown on VAT Returns, must be recorded separately in the VAT account of your business. Listings must be maintained to support both the entries and any further adjustments made to reflect subsequent amounts recovered.

Special schemes for retailers

Retailers often sell a mixture of both positive and zero-rated goods but do not know how much of each of them is sold from day to day. When this happens they can use one of the schemes available to help them work out their VAT liabilities. If you are in retailing you should study the leaflets telling you about the various schemes so that you do not pay too much tax.

Where retailers only sell goods that are liable at the standard rate of 20 per cent, the amount of tax included in the gross takings for a period is 1/6. Referred to as the 'VAT fraction', this calculation is worked out as follows:

	£		
Tax-exclusive value (say)	100.00		
Add: VAT @ 20.0 per cent	20.00		
Tax-inclusive price	£120.00		
The VAT included in the tax-inclusive price is therefore:	$\dfrac{20}{120}$	=	$\dfrac{1}{6}$

For goods liable at the reduced rate of 5 per cent the 'VAT fraction' is 1/21.

Where a retailer makes a supply for more than £250, the business must issue a proper tax invoice when asked to do so. For supplies under £250 there is usually enough information on till receipts for the 'VAT fraction' to be worked out by customers who, in the course of their business, make retail purchases and want to claim back the input tax suffered.

Flat Rate Scheme

The scheme is open to small businesses whose annual taxable turnover (not including VAT) does not exceed £150,000. It will be of particular appeal to businesses that do not want to spend too much time and effort dealing with all the administrative complications of normal VAT accounting.

Under the scheme, VAT is still charged to customers at the rate appropriate to the supplies made by the business. When you come to complete your VAT Returns:

- you do not make a separate claim to recover input tax on purchases, expenses or low-value assets acquired for your business;
- any input tax on capital assets with a value of more than £2,000, including VAT, may be claimable separately;
- you work out the tax due by applying a fixed percentage to the VAT inclusive turnover of your business for the period.

The percentages have been set by HMRC according to the principal activity of a business and take into account that input tax on normal purchases is not claimed.

Yvonne Spencer is a photographer. Her VAT inclusive turnover for the quarter to the end of March 2016 was £18,000. Yvonne must pay VAT of £2,340 as follows:

£18,000 × 13 per cent = £2,340

Businesses are being strongly encouraged by HMRC to use the scheme, so much so that a 1 per cent reduction in the percentages for the first year is available to new businesses:

- that register for VAT when they should; and
- apply to use the scheme at the same time.

You have to leave the scheme once the regular annual turnover of your business reaches a VAT inclusive amount of £230,000.

Cash accounting

Under the cash accounting scheme:

- you account for VAT on your outputs when you are paid for sales made by your business, rather than by reference to the date of your tax invoices; and
- you reclaim the VAT on your purchases and business expenses when you pay for them.

Your business is eligible to use this scheme from the beginning of a VAT tax period if:

- you expect the value of your taxable supplies (excluding VAT) during the forthcoming year to be no more than £1.35 million;
- you are not in arrears in submitting past VAT Returns at the time you decide to join the scheme.

You must come out of cash accounting if:

- the amount of your taxable supplies exceeds £1.6 million (exclusive of VAT) in a period of one year; or
- your business fails to comply with the correct requirements for record keeping.

Annual accounting

Under the annual accounting scheme your business:

- submits just one VAT Return each year;
- makes interim payments of VAT based on an estimate of your liability for the year; and
- completes and sends in its VAT Return two months after the end of the year. At the same time you pay over the balance of VAT due.

You can apply to use the scheme if you reasonably believe that the amount of your taxable supplies, excluding VAT, in the period of 12 months from the date of your application will not exceed £1.35 million. If you are accepted onto the scheme, the start date for the new arrangements will be the first day of your current accounting period. You will be notified in writing if your application has been accepted. The letter you receive will also tell you:

- the amount and timing of your interim payments; and
- the due date of the Annual Return and balancing payment.

Vince Charles is in business as a vehicle repairer and is registered for VAT. In October 2015 he applies to use the annual accounting scheme. His quarterly period runs from 1 September to 30 November. His first annual accounting period starts on 1 September 2015 and ends on 31 August 2016.

Once you are in the scheme you can remain in it until your annual turnover exceeds £1.6 million. You will then be taken off the scheme at the end of your current accounting year. Alternatively, if you want to come out of the scheme and go back to the normal method of paying and accounting for VAT you just need to tell HMRC of your decision.

Penalties, surcharges and interest

The penalty regime covering VAT aspects of your business extends to:

- failing to register for VAT on time; and
- errors in documents or Returns.

Penalties are calculated:

- as a percentage of the additional tax due; and
- when the inaccuracy is put right.

The penalty is a percentage of the extra tax due and depends on the reason for the inaccuracy as follows:

Reason	Rate of penalty	
	Maximum	**Minimum**
Reasonable care	No penalty	
Carelessness	30%	0%/10%*
Deliberate	70%	20%
Deliberate and concealed	100%	30%

As you can see there is a substantial difference between the minimum and maximum rates of penalty. Therefore, even if you have adjusted for any error on the next VAT return after it was identified you should also:

- disclose the error with full details by writing to HMRC before it is picked up by them;
- help HMRC calculate the extra VAT due; and
- allow HMRC to look at any records requested to check on the accuracy of the figures.

By doing all of this you should be able to secure a much reduced level of penalty.

Where a disclosure is made following a prompt from HMRC, the minimum levels of penalty are increased as follows:

	Rate
Carelessness	10%/20%*
Deliberate	35%
Deliberate and concealed	50%

* depending on whether the non-deliberate event took place within or after 12 months of the tax being due.

Furthermore:

- default interest, currently at a rate of 3 per cent, will normally be charged when assessments for errors are issued;
- surcharges can be imposed by HMRC where you fail to:
  - file your VAT Returns on time; and/or
  - pay the proper amount of tax when it is due.

Default surcharges:

- range from 2 per cent to 15 per cent where a history of default has built up;
- are subject to a minimum surcharge of £30;
- at the 2 per cent and 5 per cent rates are seldom assessed unless they are calculated to exceed £400.

HMRC will pay you interest in cases where they make an official error but this is currently at the rate of 0.5 per cent.

Appeals

You have the right to appeal to an independent tribunal against:

- the imposition of a penalty;
- the amount of a penalty; and
- a decision not to suspend a penalty.

Alternatively you can opt for an internal review by an independent HMRC officer. This is a quick and inexpensive way to resolve any dispute.

Complaints

VAT officers are committed to the same standards as Tax staff (see the Service Commitment reproduced in Chapter 1), and are expected to abide by them. If you ever feel dissatisfied with the manner in which the affairs of your business have been handled, or think that an officer has overstepped the mark and has exceeded his or her authority, you can write to:

- the person who is in overall charge at the HMRC office for your business; or
- the Complaints Unit for the area where your business is situated.

If you are unable to resolve your complaint satisfactorily your next step is to contact the Adjudicator's Office, which is the independent body set up specifically for this purpose.

Working for yourself

If you run your own business, other than through a company or in partnership, you are classified as self-employed for tax purposes. Your business might be a trade, profession or vocation.

Am I self-employed?

The main distinguishing factor between having self-employed status and working as an employee is the existence of a 'master–servant' relationship. Sometimes it is difficult to draw a line between:

- employment (a contract for service); and
- self-employment (a contract for services).

Your business will have the trappings of self-employment if you:

- are responsible for the success or failure of your business;
- are paid a fixed fee, or price for your work;
- can decide how, when and where the work should be undertaken;
- can dictate the hours you work;
- provide your own tools; and
- have no entitlement to paid holidays or sick leave.

You do not have to formalize any business relationship by entering into a contract for the supply of goods or services. Nevertheless, having a contract makes sound business sense because it will cover matters other than those just relative to the taxation consequences of the relationship.

Starting up in business

Your business is now up and running. It is important that you quickly learn what to do about Tax, National Insurance (see Chapter 8) and maybe Value Added Tax (see Chapter 6).

I suggest you use the online tax registration service to tell HMRC about your new business. You will find this at **www.gov.uk/new-business-register-for-tax**. As part of the registration process you will be asked if you would like to receive business advisory e-mails. HMRC recognizes that starting and running a business is challenging. By signing up for this free service you will receive a series of tax-related help and support e-mails.

Other useful services offered by HMRC include:

- free online webinar presentations allowing you to attend seminars without leaving your desk;
- e-learning which you can use whenever it suits you allowing you to learn at your own pace; and
- videos on HMRC's YouTube pages.

Records

I strongly recommend that you maintain a separate bank account for all your business income, purchases and expenses. As a minimum you should keep the following records, either electronically or manually:

- a cash book to record and analyse your sales and other receipts, purchases and overhead expenses that pass through your bank account; and
- a petty cash book to log all small transactions paid for in cash.

If you run a larger business you will probably need to maintain other accounting information as well.

Tax Saver

Whatever the size of your business it is a good discipline to:

- write up all your books of account on a regular basis; and
- maintain proper and accurate accounting records at all times.

Furthermore, in order to comply with the requirements for Self Assessment, you should keep and file the following:

- invoices for sales made by your business;
- bank statements and paying-in slips to show where the income comes from;
- invoices for goods acquired or costs incurred;
- documentation supporting purchases and sales of assets used in your business; and
- records in support of amounts taken out of the business for personal use (drawings) and all money paid into your business from personal funds (capital introduced).

Accounts

You can choose the date to which you draw up the accounts of your self-employment each year. For this reason it is unlikely that the first accounts will cover a full year of the activities of your business. You can make up your accounts from the date you start in business to the end of:

- a particular month;
- your first year's trading;
- the calendar year on 31 December; or
- the tax year.

Tax Saver

You should certainly think about your choice of accounting date. An obvious and convenient choice is 31 March as the date coincides with the end of the tax year on 5 April. However, it is sometimes preferable to go with the date early on in the tax year, such as 30 April, as it allows you more time to plan for the funding of the tax payable.

Tax Saver

Alternatively, if your business is seasonal in nature, it may be a good idea to pick an annual accounting date to coincide with the slack time of the year and when stocks are low.

Thereafter you should continue to draw up your accounts to the same date every year. You are allowed to change this date where you can show good reason to do so.

Your accounts should be drawn up to:

- work out the profit earned or loss sustained in the financial period; and

- summarize, whenever possible, on the balance sheet the amounts of the assets and liabilities at the year-end.

The statement of the profit or loss of your business is not usually the simple difference between receipts and payments. For example, if you sell to customers on credit there will inevitably be some unpaid sales at the year-end. These outstanding invoices need to come into your accounts as income for that period. Equally, where amounts are due to your suppliers for purchases or expenses at the end of your financial period these need to be included in the accounts as costs incurred in the period. If your business is:

- One that requires you to keep a stock of raw materials or finished goods, the value of that stock at the year-end must be included in the profit and loss statement as income. The basis of valuation is cost or, in the case of redundant or old stock, realizable value. The amount of your stock at the beginning of the accounting period is deductible as a cost.

- Of a professional nature or you are a service provider you must also make an adjustment to your accounts at the end of each accounting period. You must bring in as income an amount in respect of ongoing, but unbilled, work by reference to the proportion of the work completed.

When it comes to expenses make sure you claim all the overhead costs. For example:

Tax Saver

- If you are married or live with a partner and your spouse/partner helps you in the business by doing your accounts and acting as a part-time secretary or assistant, you can claim the salary paid to him/her as a business expense. You should pay a proper amount for these services. If this is his or her only job or income and the wage is less than £8,060 for the year, then there will be no tax or National Insurance to pay.

Tax Saver

- If you work from home you can claim a deduction for an appropriate proportion of the fixed costs of running your home, such as:
  - mortgage interest;
  - council tax;
  - light, heat and household insurance;
  - the rental of your landline telephone;
  - broadband;
  - general repairs and maintenance;
  - cleaning expenses.

In order to be eligible you must have a specific area in your home set aside as an office.

Tax Saver

There will be some costs of your business, such as a car used both privately and for work, when it may be difficult to apportion the expenditure between the private and business elements. Where there is this overlap, I suggest you include a note in the additional information section of the self-employed pages of your Tax Return, so your tax office can see how you have worked out the percentage of the expenditure chargeable to the business.

Tax Saver

Finally, avoid using estimates for any business expenses. If they are challenged on enquiry from HMRC you will find it difficult to substantiate what you have claimed in your accounts.

Jack Wagstaff has been in business for many years running the newsagents and confectionery shop in his local high street. He has three part-time assistants to help him in the shop.

His wife, Emily, looks after all the records of the business, pays the suppliers and completes the quarterly VAT Returns.

Jack makes up his accounts to 31 March each year. The statement of his business income and the expenses incurred during the year to 31 March 2016 are as follows:

	£	£	£
Sales			182,650
Less: Cost of Sales			
Stock of cards, sweets, stationery, cigarettes etc at start of year		2,680	
Purchases in the year		61,440	
		64,120	
Less: Stock at end of year		3,240	60,880

	£	£	£
Gross profit			121,770
Less: Overhead expenses			
Wages of part-time assistants	20,400		
Wife's salary	6,200	26,600	
Shop expenses			
Rent	22,000		
Business and Water Rates	13,750		
Light and Heat	3,800		
Insurance	820		
Cleaning	1,560		
Shop door repairs	620	42,550	
Printing postage and stationery		1,660	
Shop telephone and fax		1,790	
Computer costs		860	
Entertaining		220	
Accountancy		1,340	
Legal fees re new lease		1,260	
Car Expenses			
Road Fund Licence and insurance	720		
Petrol and oil	1,720		
Repairs and servicing	530	2,970	
Use of Home as Office (1/6 × £2,730)		455	
Home telephone		820	
Bank interest and charges		1,140	
Staff welfare		390	
Miscellaneous expenses		240	82,295
Profit for the year			£39,475

Nowadays, annual accounts of a business are often needed for reasons other than tax. For example:

- to verify income in support of an application for a mortgage; or
- by your bank manager when weighing up an application for a business loan or overdraft facility.

Cash accounting for small businesses

Alternatively, owners of small businesses can work out the annual taxable profit or loss of their business by simply deducting monies paid for supplies or expenses from income received. They do not have to make adjustments for:

- stock or work-in-progress;
- unpaid bills for either purchases or overhead expenses; or
- outstanding invoices due from customers.

The scheme is:

- optional; and
- open to all traders or professionals whose annual income is below the threshold for VAT registration.

You can elect to adopt the cash basis for 2015/16 by ticking box 10 on page SEF1 of your Tax Return.

You will have to come out of the cash basis for the year following that in which the receipts of your business exceed twice the VAT registration threshold.

Some of the other features of the cash basis are:

- adjustments are required when coming or going out of the scheme to make sure that only once:
  - is income taxed; and
  - payments are deducted.
- payments for interest up to £500 each year are allowed. It does not matter whether the interest is on a loan for either business or private purposes;
- monies spent on buying plant and machinery, but not cars, are deductable against income of the business.

> **Tax Saver**
>
> Losses incurred can be carried forward to be set against profits of future years. However, losses cannot be carried back or set off against other income. This restriction on tax relief for losses could be a significant disadvantage to some businesses.

Fixed rate deduction scheme

You can also use optional simplified flat rate calculations to work out some of your business expenses. The main types of expenditure covered are those relating to:

- cars, vans or motor cycles. For each vehicle the costs included in the fixed deduction cover both the purchase and all running costs. Once the fixed rate scheme has been used for a vehicle it is compulsory for each subsequent period that the vehicle is used in the business. The allowable rates for 2015/16 are:

	For each of the first 10,000 business miles	For each business mile over 10,000
Cars and goods vehicles	45p	25p
Motorcycles	24p	24p

- the use of your home. You can deduct a fixed monthly rate which depends on the number of hours you, or any of your employees, spend working at your home. The monthly rates of deduction for 2015/16 are:

Number of hours worked per month	Allowable amount
25 or more	£10
51 or more	£18
101 or more	£26

However, this flat rate does not include the proportion of your telephone or internet used for your business. You can claim these expenses by working out the actual costs incurred.

Tax Return information

If you were in business at any time during the 2015/16 tax year you will need to complete the supplementary self-employment pages to accompany your Tax Return for the year. The self-employment pages are in a set format for reporting the annual income and expenses of your business. Your Return will not be accepted as complete if the information about your business income and expenses is not presented in the required format.

When Jack Wagstaff comes to complete the supplementary self-employment pages for the year ended 5 April 2016 he will fill in the section on business income and expenses, based on his accounts for the financial year to 31 March 2016, as follows:

	£
Sales/business income (excluding VAT)	**182,650**
Total expenses	
Cost of goods bought for re-sale or goods used	60,880
Payments to subcontractors	–
Wages, salaries and other staff costs	26,600
Car, van and travel expenses	2,970
Rent, rates, power and insurance costs	40,825
Repairs and renewals of property and equipment	620
Telephone, fax, stationery and other office costs	5,830
Advertising and business entertainment costs	220
Interest on bank and other loans	1,140
Bank credit card and other financial charges	–
Irrecoverable debts written off	–
Accountancy, legal and other professional fees	2,600
Other finance charges	–
Depreciation and loss/(profit) on sale of assets	–
Other business expenses	1,490
Total expenses	**143,175**
Net profit	**£39,475**

	£
Notes:	
(1) Wages, salaries and other staff costs are:	
Part-time assistants	20,400
Wife's salary	6,200
	26,600
(2) Rent rates, power and insurance costs are:	
Shop expenses (excluding cleaning and door repairs)	40,370
Use of home as office	455
	40,825
(3) Telephone, fax, stationery and other office costs are:	
Printing, postage and stationery	1,660
Telephone (shop and home)	2,610
Shop cleaning	1,560
	5,830
(4) Accountancy, legal and other professional costs are:	
Accountancy	1,340
Legal fees	1,260
	2,600
(5) Other business expenses:	
Computer costs	860
Staff welfare	390
Miscellaneous expenses	240
	1,490

So as to minimize the risk of HMRC raising enquiries into your self-employment income and Tax Return, you should adopt a consistent pattern from year to year in the way you analyse your business expenses under the various headings of the standardized format.

If the annual turnover of your business was below £82,000:

- you only need to complete the self-employment (short) supplementary pages; and

- you can add up all your business expenses allowable for tax purposes and just enter the total figure in Box 19 on page SES1.

Profits for tax

The profit disclosed by your business accounts will not necessarily be the same as that on which your tax bill is calculated. This is because certain types of expenditure are specifically not allowable in working out taxable business profits. These include:

- goods or materials bought for personal use;
- the private proportion of mixed expenses;
- business entertainment;
- non-business charitable donations;
- amounts spent on items of a capital nature;
- professional costs related to capital expenditure, such as the legal expenses of buying property;
- own wages or drawings; and
- general provisions and reserves.

Although Jack Wagstaff's accounts for his financial year to 31 March 2016 show he made a profit of £39,475, his taxable profit is £43,311 as follows:

		£	£
Profit as per accounts			39,475
Add:	Disallowable expenses		
	Private proportion of car expenses (60 per cent)	1,782	
	Private proportion of home telephone (70 per cent)	574	
	Entertainment	220	
	Legal fees re new lease	1,260	
			3,836
Profit as adjusted for tax purposes			£43,311

Profits of the tax year

Self-employed individuals are taxed on the profits of their financial year ending in the tax year. This is known as 'the basis period'.

> The tax-adjusted profit of £43,311 for the year to 31 March 2016 of Jack Wagstaff's high-street business will be taxed in 2015/16.

There are special rules for working out the profits on which you pay tax in the opening years of your business, as follows:

- in the first tax year your taxable profits are those arising in the period from commencement to the following 5 April;
- if you choose to prepare your business accounts up to a date 12 months after you began your business then, in the second tax year, you pay tax on the profits for the first full year of trading; and
- for the third and all subsequent tax years you pay tax on the profits for 'the basis period'.

Under these rules it is usual for the profits for some periods of account to be taken into account more than once in working out the amount on which you pay tax. However, over the lifetime of your business it is intended that the profits should be taxed in full but once and once only. As a result, profits that are taxed more than once are eligible for a special relief. Known as overlap relief it will be given when either:

- a business ceases; or
- for any earlier tax year where the basis period exceeds 12 months.

James Gray started up in business on 1 May 2015. His annual accounting date is 30 April. He makes the following profits in the first two years:

Year to 30/04/2016	£24,720
Year to 30/04/2017	£28,360

The taxable profits for the first three tax years are:

Tax year	Basis period	Taxable profit (£)
2015/16	01/05/2015 to 05/04/2016	22,660
2016/17	Year to 30/04/2016	24,720
2017/18	Year to 30/04/2017	28,360

On cessation the taxable profits for the final tax year will be:

- those earned in the period from the end of the basis period in the previous tax year up to cessation, but reduced by overlap relief.

James Gray decides to close down his business on 30 April 2023. In the final year James makes profits of £34,950. The final tax year is 2023/24 and James will pay tax on:

	£
Taxable profit of final year	34,950
Less: Overlap, 01/05/2015 to 05/04/2016	22,660
Net taxable amount	£12,290

Special rules apply when a business changes its accounting date. Apart from the first and last years of business, the profits of a 12-month period are taxed in each tax year.

Sheila Windows began her business on 1 December 2015. She draws up her first accounts to 30 November 2016 and makes a profit of £33,000. She then decides to change her accounting date by extending it to 31 January 2018. The accounts for this 14-month period show a taxable profit of £28,000. Her basis period and taxable profits for the opening years of the business are:

Tax year	Basis period	Taxable profit (£)
2015/16	01/12/2015 to 05/04/2016	11,000
2016/17	Year to 30/11/2016	33,000
The overlap period is from 01/12/2015 to 05/04/2016:		
2017/18	01/12/2016 to 31/01/2018 (14 months)	28,000
Less: Overlap	01/12/2015 to 31/01/2016	5,500
Net taxable amount		£22,500

The overlap period was one of four months. As the accounting period from 1 December 2016 to 31 January 2018 is 14 months, the overlap is a period of two months. The amount deducted from the taxable profits for 2017/18 is half of the original overlap profit. A further two months of overlap relief is available either when the business ceases or in any subsequent tax year when the basis period is again longer than 12 months.

Pre-trading and post-cessation expenses

Any expenditure which you incurred in the seven years before you started to trade is:

- treated as if it was spent on the first day of business; and
- tax deductible.

The relief only extends to those costs and other outgoings which would qualify for tax relief had they been incurred on the first day of trading.

Tax relief is also allowed on certain expenditure incurred after your business has ceased. The expenses that qualify for relief are:

- those closely related to the trading or professional activities previously carried on; and

- including, for example, relief for debts that have subsequently proved to be irrecoverable.

Relief is available for payments made within seven years of the permanent discontinuance of the business by setting the payments made against income for the same tax year. Any excess can be treated as a capital loss, but only of the same tax year.

Capital allowances

You can claim what are known as capital allowances on the expenditure you incur on items of a capital nature for your business.

Amounts spent by businesses attract the following rates of allowance in the first year:

- 100 per cent on annual expenditure up to £200,000* on most types of plant and machinery;

- 100 per cent on most energy-saving or environmentally beneficial plant and machinery;

- 100 per cent for purchases of new low-emission cars for use by you or your staff in your business (to qualify a car must not emit more than 75gm/km CO_2 or be electrically propelled);

- 100 per cent on the purchase of new electric vans; and

- 18 per cent for cars with CO_2 emissions above 75g/km but not exceeding 130g/km (this rate reduces to 8 per cent for cars exceeding this CO_2 emission limit).

* this limit took effect on 1 January 2016. Previously it was £500,000.

Tax Saver

It may be tax efficient to incur capital expenditure towards the end of an accounting year rather than early in the following year. You will then benefit from any of the above first year allowances due on the expenditure at an earlier date.

In subsequent years your capital expenditure, after deducting your first year allowances, is further written down on the reducing-balance basis.

A separate 'pool' must be maintained for expenditure in each of the following different categories:

- all plant and equipment, including motor vans, lorries and cars with CO_2 emissions of 130g/km* or less;
- all cars with CO_2 emissions exceeding 160g/km;
- each asset where there is both business and personal use; and
- each asset with a short life expectancy.

* 160g/km for purchases before 6 April 2013.

The rates of allowance are:

- 18 per cent per annum; or
- 8 per cent per annum for cars purchased from 6 April 2009 onwards and with CO_2 emissions exceeding 130g/km*.

* 160g/km for purchases before 6 April 2013.

Where the unrelieved expenditure is no more than £1,000 you can claim tax relief on the full amount.

Where an asset on which capital allowances have been claimed is sold, you must bring the proceeds of sale into the computation of capital allowances. If it is sold for less than the value to which it has been written down for tax purposes you will probably be entitled to a further allowance equivalent to the difference between the sale proceeds and the written-down value.

These adjustments are respectively known as balancing allowances and balancing charges.

In his accounting year to 31 March 2016 Jack Wagstaff traded in his old car for £2,400 and bought a new one with a CO$_2$ emission limit of 120g/km for £20,000. In the year he also spent £3,100 on fittings for his shop, £1,400 on a computer and printer and £200 on a new office filing cabinet. His claim to capital allowances for 2015/16, based on his capital expenditure in this year, is:

	(£)	Pool (£)	Car with private use (£)
Written-down values brought forward from 2014/15		6,300	4,100
Sale proceeds of car			2,400
Balancing allowance			£1,700
Additions in the year:			
Shop fittings, computer and cabinet		4,700	
New car			20,000
		11,000	
Allowances due:			
Annual Investment – 100 per cent	4,700		
Writing down – 18 per cent	1,134	5,834	3,600
Carried forward to 2016/17		£5,166	£16,400
Summary of allowances:			
Annual Investment		4,700	
Writing down		4,734	
Balancing		1,700	
		11,134	
Less: 60 per cent private use of car		3,180	
2015/16 Capital allowances		£7,954	

Capital allowances are deducted from your profits as a trading expense of your business. Any balancing charges are treated as an addition to your profit. It follows that:

- the chargeable period for the purposes of working out your capital allowances is the same as that for which you draw up your accounts; and

- the length of the period of account determines the amount of writing-down allowances to which you are entitled.

Thus, if a period of account:

- is only nine months long, 9/12th of the writing-down allowances can be deducted from taxable profits for that period; or

- extends to 15 months, the tax deductible allowances equal 15/12th of the writing-down allowances.

Should a period of account exceed 18 months, it must be divided into one of 12 months and a balancing period with restricted writing-down allowances.

There is a section in the supplementary self-employment pages in which you must summarize your claim to capital allowances.

Losses

> **Tax Saver**
>
> It is almost inevitable that your business will go through both good and bad times. If so, you need to be aware of, and to consider, all of the different options for claiming the tax relief due on the loss.

If you incur a loss you can claim tax relief on the loss sustained as increased by the amount of your capital allowances for the same period. You can choose whether to set a trading loss against other income in either the same, or the preceding, tax year. But you cannot claim to relieve only part of a loss.

> Isabel Fletcher has been in business for many years. She makes up her accounts to 31 August each year. In the year ended 31 August 2016 she makes a loss that she can claim against her other income in 2016/17. Alternatively, the loss can be carried back and relieved against her total income in 2015/16.

Any unrelieved loss of your business then has to be carried forward for offset against profits from the same business in future years.

Alternatively you can claim to set a trading loss against capital gains (see Chapter 13) in the following way:

- The claim is for relief on the amount of the trading loss that cannot be set against your other income in the year or on which tax relief has already been given in some other way.
- The maximum loss eligible for relief against capital gains is the same as the amount of your gains chargeable to Capital Gains Tax.

It is not possible to make a partial claim.

Tax Saver

> By relieving a business loss this way you may be wasting personal allowances as well as your annual exemption for Capital Gains Tax.

Tax relief for losses incurred by new businesses is extended such that:

- Losses incurred during the first four tax years can be set against your total income for the three years prior to that in which the loss arises.
- Relief is first of all given against total income for the earliest year. For example, if you set up in business during 2015/16 and sustained a loss in the first period of trading, that part of the loss attributable to the 2015/16 tax year can be set against your income in 2012/13, 2013/14 and 2014/15, beginning with 2012/13.

There is one final type of loss relief that is only available to those businesses that incur a loss in their last period of trading. In such circumstances there cannot be future profits against which such a loss might be relieved. Therefore, a loss arising in the last 12 months of trading can be set back against the profits from the same business in both the final and three preceding tax years, beginning with the profits of the last year and working backwards.

Ralph Collins retires from business on 30 September 2016. In the final nine months in business he loses £18,000. Previously his business had always been successful as follows:

Accounting year	Taxable profits (£)	Year of charge
Year ended 31 December 2012	16,000	2012/13
Year ended 31 December 2013	12,000	2013/14
Year ended 31 December 2014	9,000	2014/15
Year ended 31 December 2015	4,000	2015/16

The terminal loss can be set off as follows:

2015/16	£4,000	leaving nil taxable profits
2014/15	£9,000	leaving nil taxable profits
2013/14	£5,000	reducing the taxable profits to £7,000
	£18,000	

Limit of reliefs

There is a limit on the amount of certain income tax reliefs that you can claim. This annual 'cap' is the greater limit of:

- £50,000; or

- 25 per cent of your total income.

The reliefs caught by this rule include:

- claiming to set off early year, annual or post-cessation trading losses against other income, but not capital gains; and

- qualifying loan interest (Chapter 4).

> In 2015/16 Ben Turner suffered a loss of £60,000 in his business. Ben made a claim to offset this loss against his total income for the year of £140,000. The maximum loss that can be relieved is £50,000 as this is more than £35,000 (25 per cent of Ben's income of £140,000).

The restriction of relief for business losses may have a significant adverse impact on the finances of owners of any small or medium-sized businesses:

- suffering a blip in profitability; or

- investing in plant or machinery to take advantage of the £200,000 Annual Investment Limit.

Taking on staff

You have now reached the time where your business is expanding. You need an assistant or an extra pair of hands. When you start employing staff you need to register:

- as an employer with HMRC; and

- before the first payday.

I suggest you do this online.

As an employer you are responsible for:

- Working out the deductions for Income Tax (PAYE) and National Insurance Contributions from the salary or wage paid to your employees at regular weekly or monthly intervals.

- Paying over the deductions to the Collector of Taxes each month. These payments can be made every quarter where your average monthly payments of PAYE and National Insurance Contributions are less than £1,500.

- Letting your tax office know every year how much each employee has earned together with the deductions made for both Income Tax and National Insurance Contributions. The deductions should reconcile to the total of the amounts paid over to the Collector of Taxes. You must also give details of any benefits paid or provided.

- Giving your employees certificates showing their earnings for the tax year, deductions for Income Tax and National Insurance Contributions and the value of any benefits provided.

Some other ways to save on tax

Tax Saver

Look into taking your spouse/partner into partnership where he or she helps you in the business and your annual profits are such that the top slice is taxable at the higher 40 per cent or additional 45 per cent rates. Between you it may be possible to make significant savings in your overall annual tax bill.

Tax Saver

If your business is growing and becoming ever more profitable you should seriously think about transferring it to a limited company with the following advantages:

- The rate of tax paid by a company on its profits is much lower than the corresponding Income Tax rates on personal income.

- The members' liability is limited to the amount paid for their shares and any loans to the company.

- Once formed a company can exist forever.

- No other person can use the company name.

- New shareholders and investors can easily be introduced.

Finally, when you want to retire it is far easier to:

- Sell your stake in a company; or

- Transfer ownership of your shares,

than sell, or pass on, a business operating as a sole trader.

Tax Saver

Finally, always look to the future and plan for your retirement, whether you are contemplating a sale of your business or handing it down to the next generation.

Foster carers

Those who receive income from local authorities or independent fostering providers for providing foster care to children and young people, or are qualified shared-lives carers are entitled to a special relief, which comes in two parts:

- an exemption from Income Tax on receipts that do not exceed the qualifying amount for any year; and
- a simplified optional method of calculating taxable profits where receipts are more than the qualifying amount.

The annual qualifying amount is made up of two parts, which must be added together. They are:

- a fixed amount for each household – £10,000 for 2015/16; and
- a weekly amount for each foster-child placed with you – for 2015/16, £200 a week for a child under age 11 and £250 a week for a child over 11 years old.

Mollie Ford, who lives on her own, provides foster care for two boys during 2015/16. The 12-year-old is only with her for 16 weeks but the 9-year-old boy stays with her for the whole year. Her qualifying amount for 2015/16 is £24,400 calculated as follows:

	£
Fixed amount	10,000
9-year-old (52 weeks × £200)	10,400
12-year-old (16 weeks × £250)	4,000
2015/16 qualifying amount	24,400

Where your receipts (fees, salaries, reward payments, allowances, etc) exceed the annual qualifying amount you can choose between paying tax on:

- your actual profits from foster caring, worked out on the principles that apply for any other business; or
- profits worked out on a simplified method, which is the difference between your total receipts for the year less the annual qualifying amount.

Whichever way you choose to be taxed you must at least keep records of your receipts and the ages and number of weeks that you care for each child placed with you. For this purpose a week runs from Monday to the following Sunday. Part of a week counts as a full week.

Furnished holiday accommodation

The letting of furnished holiday accommodation in both the United Kingdom and anywhere else in the European Economic Area may be treated as a trade as long as the property is:

- let commercially and furnished;
- available for letting commercially to the public as holiday accommodation for at least 210 days in a 12-month period; and
- actually let for at least 105 such days.

Any period exceeding 31 days during which the property is occupied by the same person does not count towards the 105 days test.

If, in any 12-month period, the periods of occupation of more than 31 days total more than 155 days the accommodation will not qualify under these rules.

As the letting of furnished holiday accommodation is treated as a trading activity:

- you can claim capital allowances on expenditure for furniture and equipment in the holiday home; but you can only claim relief for losses, including mortgage interest, against income from your furnished holiday-letting business.

Other special situations

In the space available I have only been able to paint a general picture of the way in which the profits of most businesses are taxed. If you are a farmer, a writer, a Lloyds underwriter or a subcontractor in the construction industry, you should know that there are special rules for working out the taxable profits from these and some other trades, professions or vocations. In such situations it is advisable to seek professional assistance.

National Insurance and state benefits

08

Employed or self-employed, you must pay National Insurance Contributions as well as Income Tax on your earnings or business profits. By paying sufficient National Insurance Contributions you become eligible to claim those social security benefits that are based on your contribution history. Many benefits, mainly those payable to the disabled, do not depend upon the payment of contributions.

National Insurance numbers

You need to have a National Insurance number (NINO) so that all the contributions you make can be properly recorded. It is unique to you and made up of two letters and six numbers, followed by a further letter – A, B, C or D. You keep the same number for your whole life.

All children are notified of their NINO shortly before their 16th birthday providing:

- they live in the UK; and
- their parents or guardians are receiving Child Benefit for them.

Or else you can apply at any time over the age of 16:

- in order to claim tax credits and/or benefits;
- when you start in employment or working for yourself; or
- if you have applied for a student loan.

If any of these circumstances apply, and you are under 20 years old, you should contact the National Insurance Registrations Helpline on 0300 200 3502. Otherwise, you should call the National Insurance number application line on 0345 600 0643.

National Insurance Contributions

There are four classes of contribution payable as follows:

- Class 1 by employees;
- Class 2 by the self-employed;
- Classes 3 and 3A, which are voluntary; and
- Class 4 by the self-employed, based on profits of your business.

The rates of National Insurance Contributions for 2015/16 are listed in Appendix 4 on page 264.

You do not have to go on paying contributions once you attain State Pension age, even if you carry on working either in employment or in your own business. For a man this is currently age 65. For women born between 6 April 1950 and 5 April 1955 there is a gradual increase in State Pension age from ages 60 to 65.

(a) Class 1

The earnings of employees on which contributions are calculated include:

- a salary or wage – before deduction for pension contributions;
- overtime, bonuses and commission;
- holiday pay; and
- statutory sick, maternity and paternity pay.

No contributions are payable by employees on:

- business expenses;
- tips and gratuities; or
- redundancy payments.

The contributions you pay are usually a percentage of your weekly or monthly salary or wage, subject to lower and upper-earnings limits that change from year to year. The rate and amount of contribution you pay when you return to work is unaffected if:

- you change jobs and have a break between them; or
- there is a period when you are unemployed.

Tax Saver

If you have more than one employment you must pay contributions on your earnings from all your jobs. However, there is an overall annual maximum limit of contributions payable by employees. You can apply for a refund in any year where the total contributions you have paid exceed this annual limit. Alternatively, by completing form CA72A, you can apply for deferment where you reckon that the contributions you will pay on earnings from two or more employments will exceed the maximum annual limit. The National Insurance Contributions and Employer Office of HMRC will then instruct one or other of your employers not to withhold contributions from your earnings. After the end of the tax year your overall contribution history is reviewed. If you have not paid enough contributions the National Insurance Contributions Office will send you a calculation and a demand for the balance due.

(b) Class 2

This is a weekly flat rate payable by the self-employed. They are collected through the tax system with both Income Tax and Class 4 contributions.

If your business profits are less than a specified limit each year (£5,965 for 2015/16) you are exempted from paying contributions. But you should apply in advance for what is known as small-earnings exception.

(c) Class 3

The payment of these flat-rate contributions is voluntary. It may sometimes be beneficial to pay Class 3 contributions, such as when you have been:

- in a job but your wage was below the lower earnings limit;
- abroad; or
- in prison.

But there are usually time limits for the payment of contributions in such circumstances.

(d) Class 3A

Individuals who become entitled to a State Pension before 6 April 2016 can pay the new voluntary Class 3A contributions to top up their State Pension by between £1 and £25 per week. The chance to pay this top up:

- only lasts until 5 April 2017;
- is targeted at pensioners such as the self-employed and women who have not fared so well under the State Pension rules to 5 April 2016; and
- want to enhance their retirement income by purchasing additional State Pension.

However, this is not for everyone. For example, if you are single or suffer from ill health. A long life is key as your estate will not receive any monies when you die.

To work out:

- what lump sum you can afford to pay; and
- how much additional State Pension this will buy,

visit the Government's web page at **www.gov.uk/state-pension-topup**. Alternatively, you can telephone 0345 600 4270.

(e) Class 4

These are payable by the self-employed based on a percentage of taxable business profits, after capital allowances, but before relief for pension contributions. They are paid each year through self assessment along with the Income Tax due on business profits.

The profits of Jack Wagstaff's business, as adjusted for tax purposes, are £43,311 for 2015/16. For the same year his claim to capital allowances amounts to £7,954, giving a net chargeable amount of £35,357 for 2015/16. He pays Class 4 National Insurance Contributions of £2,456.73 as follows:

	£	£
On the first	8,060	Nil
On the next	27,297 @ 9 per cent	2,456.73
		2,456.73

Tax Saver

You do not have to pay if you:

- are under 16 years old; or

- reach pension age before the start of the tax year.

Social Security benefits

Responsibility for administering all aspects of the Social Security system lies with the Department for Work and Pensions (DWP). There are local DWP offices all across the country. The framework of the Social Security system is now so substantial, and the range of benefits so wide and varied, that it is only possible for me to give a brief summary of the main state benefits that fall into these categories:

- working-age benefits (for those under the age of 60), administered by Jobcentre Plus;

- pension-age benefits (for those over the age of 60), administered by the Pension, Disability and Carers Service;

- tax credits (see Chapter 3) for families with children and people in work, administered by HMRC; and

- disability and carer benefits, administered by the Pension, Disability and Carers Service.

Many benefits are only payable to individuals with an established National Insurance contribution history. The type of benefit you can claim depends on the class of contributions paid as follows:

Type of benefit	Class 1 (Employed)	Class 2 (Self-employed)	Class 3 (Voluntary)
Retirement Pension			
– basic	Yes	Yes	Yes
– additional	Yes	No	No
– widow's	Yes	Yes	Yes
Bereavement allowance	Yes	Yes	Yes
Bereavement payment	Yes	Yes	Yes
Widowed mother's allowance	Yes	Yes	Yes
Widowed parent's allowance	Yes	Yes	Yes
Widow's payment	Yes	Yes	Yes
Incapacity benefit	Yes	Yes	No
Jobseeker's allowance	Yes	No	No
Employment and support allowance	Yes	Yes	No
Statutory sick, maternity and paternity pay	Yes	No	No
Shared parental pay	Yes	No	No
Maternity allowance	No	No	No

Other benefits do not depend upon the payment of contributions.

(a) Statutory sick pay

To be able to claim statutory sick pay you must be paying sufficient Class 1 contributions. Other main points are:

- it is a flat-rate cash payment made to employees by their employer;
- to claim you must be both incapable of work and not actually do any work at all on the day in question;

- it is not payable for the first three agreed qualifying days in any period when you are too unwell to work; and
- in any period of sickness you have a maximum entitlement to 28 weeks of statutory sick pay.

(b) Statutory maternity pay

Eligibility for statutory maternity pay is again dependent on the payment of Class 1 contributions. A woman:

- qualifies for statutory maternity pay if she has been working continuously for the same employer for 26 weeks up to, and including, the 15th week before her baby is due;
- must provide evidence of being pregnant and give her employer sufficient notice of leaving work; and
- will receive benefit for 39 weeks beginning not earlier than the 11th week before the baby is due, although she can actually select the time over which she will be absent from work.

(c) Statutory paternity pay

The basic features of ordinary statutory paternity pay are:

- fathers are allowed up to two weeks away from work during the first eight weeks of their child's life;
- it is also a flat-rate cash payment; and
- the qualifying requirements are the same as those for statutory maternity pay.

(d) Shared parental leave and pay

Additional statutory paternity pay:

- allows parents to swap the role of the main carer of their child; and
- is only payable during the mother's 39 week maternity allowance, statutory maternity pay period.

There must still be at least two weeks of this pay period remaining when the mother returns to work.

(e) Jobseeker's Allowance

The key points of the Jobseeker's Allowance, which is taxable, are:

- entitlement is based on either a satisfactory contribution record or a means-tested low income;

- it is payable to unemployed individuals between the ages of 18 and state pension age who are not in full-time education, available for work and are actively seeking employment;

- a claimant must sign a claimant commitment, which is an agreement to complete certain tasks; for example, making a work plan;

- it is a weekly benefit with supplements for age and other personal circumstances; and

- an individual is disqualified from receiving benefit if he or she fails to keep to the claimant commitment or does not carry out something requested by a work coach or employment scheme provider.

(f) Employment and Support Allowance

Employment and Support Allowance helps people with ill health and disability to move into work. It has replaced Incapacity Benefit and Income Support paid because of an illness or disability.

You may be able to claim this allowance if any of the following apply:

- you are no longer receiving Statutory Sick Pay or you cannot get it;

- you are not getting Jobseeker's Allowance;

- you have been receiving Statutory Maternity Pay and have not gone back to work because of illness or a disability;

- you are self-employed and unemployed; and

- you are under State Pension age.

You must also either:

- have had an illness or disability that stops you from working for at least four days in a row (weekends and public holidays also count);

- be unable to work for two or more days out of seven consecutive days; or

- be getting special medical treatment.

If you are between 16 and 20 years old (or under 25 if you were in education or training for at least three months immediately before you turned 20), you must:

- have been unable to work because of an illness or disability lasting at least 28 weeks; and
- have not been able to work before you turned 20 (or 25 if you were in education or training for at least three months immediately before turning 20).

There are two types of Employment and Support allowance:

- contribution-based; and
- income-related.

To be able to claim the contribution-based type:

- you must have paid enough National Insurance Contributions; and
- payment is limited to one year.

You may be able to claim income-related Employment and Support Allowance:

- if you do not have enough money coming in; or
- if you have not paid enough National Insurance Contributions and you satisfy the entitlement conditions.

(g) Income support

Income support is a non-contributory weekly benefit paid to individuals who do not have sufficient money to live on. The circumstances of each individual are looked at and the amounts required to meet their weekly needs are assessed. These are food, fuel, water rates, ordinary clothing and housing costs.

(h) Universal Credit

Universal Credit:

- is being introduced in stages;
- to replace existing benefits; and
- is exempt from tax.

What you will get depends on both your income and circumstances. It can include assistance:

- for children and childcare;
- for housing;
- if you suffer from ill health or are disabled; and
- for looking after someone with a disability.

(i) Child benefit

Child benefit is payable:

- to individuals bringing up children;
- for all children under 16 years old; and
- for children over age 16, but under 19, providing they are still in full-time education, which includes courses at school or college up to A-level.

It is not means-tested and for couples who are married it is the mother who should make the claim.

High-income households receiving Child Benefit are subject to a tax charge (see Chapter 11).

(j) Personal Independence Payment

To be eligible for a Personal Independence Payment (PIP) you must:

- be aged 16 to 64;
- have a long-term health condition or disability; and
- have difficulties with daily living activities or mobility.

PIP:

- was introduced in April 2013 for new claimants;
- is tax free; and
- comprises standard and enhanced components for both the daily living and mobility components.

Gradually PIP will replace the disability living allowance currently paid to claimants of this allowance.

(k) Attendance allowance

Attendance allowance is paid to people over the age of 65 who:

- are seriously disabled, mentally or physically; and
- need a lot of care and attention both throughout the day and at night.

Capital limits

If your capital is over £16,000, you will not be entitled to:

- Universal Credit;
- Income Support;
- Housing Benefit; or
- Income-related Jobseeker's and Employment and Support allowances.

The amount of the above benefits you will receive is tapered where your capital is between £6,000 and £16,000. Capital includes:

- cash;
- funds held in a bank or building society account; and
- shares or investment trusts at market value or surrender rate less 10 per cent.

Cap on benefits

The amount that individuals can now receive in benefits is limited to:

- £500 a week for couples;
- £500 a week for single parents whose children live with them;
- £350 a week for single adults.

The 'cap' applies to the combined amounts of:

- Jobseeker's Allowance.
- Incapacity Benefit.
- Income Support.
- Employment and Support Allowance.

- Housing Benefit.
- Child Benefit.
- Child Tax Credit and other benefits.
- Bereavement, Carers, Guardians, Maternity and Severe Disablement Allowances.

Some households including those with someone receiving:

- Personal Independence Payment;
- Disability Living Allowance;
- Attendance Allowance; or
- The Support component of the Employment and Support Allowance,

are exempt, as are war widows, widowers and households with someone entitled to the Working Tax Credit.

Benefits and rates

Listed in Appendix 5 on page 265 are all the Social Security benefits, distinguishing between those that are taxable and non-taxable.

Following on (page 267) is Appendix 6, which gives the rates of the main Social Security benefits for 2015/16.

State Pension Credit

An individual is entitled to the State Pension Credit if he or she:

- lives in Great Britain;
- satisfies at least one of two requirements of the guarantee and savings credits respectively; and
- has reached the qualifying age.

Tax Saver

The guarantee credit 'tops up' the income of a single claimant to £151.20 per week for 2015/16. For couples, including civil partners, the weekly income limit increases to £230.85.

A claimant's income includes:

- a state and any other pension;
- earnings;
- some Social Security benefits; and
- notional investment income of £1 a week for every £500 of savings or capital in excess of £10,000 (excluding your home and possessions).

The purpose of the savings credit, the rules for which are far from simple, is to reduce Pension Credit by 40 per cent of the amount by which a pensioner's income exceeds the appropriate minimum guarantee.

The guarantee credit is available to:

- both men and women who have reached the State Pension age for women; and
- a member of a couple where the other partner has attained the State Pension age for women.

The qualifying age for both men and women increases to age 65 for the savings credit element.

State and private pensions

09

I don't doubt that when you give up work and retire you will want to be able to maintain your lifestyle and living standards. You may have built up savings while you were working but your income in retirement is most likely to come from:

- the State Pension; and
- an employer or personal pension scheme.

So that you can give yourself the best possible opportunity to build up a good pension you should start contributing to a plan as soon as you can reasonably afford to do so.

State pension

There are four parts to the State Retirement Pension:

- the basic retirement (or old person's) pension;
- a state-earnings-related pension (SERPS/S2P);
- a graduated pension; and
- the age addition if you are over 80.

(a) Basic state pension

You are entitled to a basic pension if you:

- have reached state pension age;
- satisfy the contribution requirements; and
- make a claim for the pension.

State pension age for men is age 65. For women, there is a progressive increase from age 60 to 65 depending on their date of birth between 6 April 1950 and 5 April 1955.

To receive a full basic state pension you need 30 qualifying years. Otherwise you will receive a basic pension equivalent to 1/30th of the weekly rate for each of your qualifying years.

A qualifying year is a tax year in which you have earned, or been credited with, earnings equivalent to at least 52 × the lower weekly earnings limit for National Insurance purposes.

It may be possible for a married woman to use her husband's contributions to improve the amount of her State Pension. Similarly contributions made by a married man or civil partner might enhance her husband's or civil partner's State Pension respectively.

In any year you receive certain Social Security benefits, you will be credited with earnings up to the amount to make that year a qualifying year.

(b) SERPS/S2P

As the name implies any entitlement to the state second pension depends on your earnings while you are working and the payment of Class 1 contributions.

The additional state pension, when it was first introduced in 1978, was known as SERPS. It was reformed in 2002 as S2P to provide a more generous additional state pension for individuals on low or moderate incomes.

(c) A graduated pension

You will have earned extra state pension if you paid graduated National Insurance Contributions when the scheme was in operation between April 1961 and April 1975.

(d) Married or in a Civil Partnership

If you are:

- not eligible for a basic State Pension; or
- are not receiving the full rate

you might be able to qualify or 'top up' to £69.50 a week by reference to the National Insurance Contributions paid by your spouse or civil partner.

You must have both reached State Pension age and your spouse or civil partner:

- qualifies for some basic State Pension; and
- was born on or after 6 April 1950 (although this rule does not apply to married women).

(e) Death

If your spouse or civil partner is:

- over State Pension age on your death; and
- not getting the full State Pension,

they may be able to increase their pension based on your qualifying years.

But if they have not yet reached State Pension age when you die any entitlement you have built up will be included in their own State Pension. However:

- they must not have re-married; or
- formed a new civil partnership,

by the time they attain State Pension age.

Lump sums

You can defer taking your State Pension and either:

- receive an increased pension when you actually take it; or
- be paid a lump sum.

If you opt for a simple addition to your future State Pension, the higher weekly payment is the amount that is taxable when you start to receive it.

Tax Saver

Sometimes it can make sense to defer taking your State Pension in return for a lump sum at a later date. You might be in a lower tax bracket when you receive the lump sum for the deferred pension.

Under the lump sum alternative:

- the rate of pension is that fixed at the time you apply for deferral;
- the single payment will comprise both pension arrears, including increments, and interest thereon;
- the total amount is liable to income tax;
- it is not added to income for any tax purposes;
- it does not impact on the calculation of the amount of either the age-related personal or married couple's allowances;

- the tax you pay on the lump sum is worked out by applying your marginal rate of tax;
- the Pension Service will deduct tax at source based on your declaration indicating your likely band of taxable income;
- you can elect for it to be paid and, therefore, taxed in the following tax year;
- you can do this at any time from the date you choose to receive the lump sum up to one month later;
- no further interest is added to the lump sum;
- the minimum deferral period is one of 12 consecutive months; there is no maximum length of time for which drawing your State Pension can be deferred; and
- in most cases the executors of a deceased persons estate will be able to claim any undrawn lump sum benefit that had accrued up to the date of death.

Archie Barber is now in his late 60s. He was entitled to draw his State Pension in June 2014 but decided against doing so at the time. He chose to take his lump sum, amounting to £6,240, one year later in June 2015. In 2015/16 his total pension income amounted to £19,000 and he received gross interest on his building society account of £800. He pays tax of £1,248 on his lump sum as follows:

	£
Pensions	19,000
Building Society interest	800
	19,800
Less: Personal age allowance	10,600
Taxable income	9,200
2015/16 tax due: £9,200 × 20 per cent	1,840
Tax payable on lump sum State Pension: £6,240 × 20 per cent (as a 20 per cent tax payer)	£1,248

State Pension forecast

As you approach retirement age, for State Pension purposes it is a good idea to get a forecast of what you will receive from the DWP.

You can get a State Pension forecast if you are more than 30 days away from state pension age when your application is processed. Your forecast will advise you in today's money of:

- how much State Pension you may get; and
- the number of qualifying years on your National Insurance record.

The application form BR19 is available from the Pension Service by telephoning 0345 3000 168. Alternatively, the forecast can be obtained online.

The new State Pension

If you reach the State Pension age after 5 April 2016 you are eligible for the new State Pension.

You qualify if you are:

- a man born after 6 April 1951; or
- a woman born after 6 April 1953.

The full new State Pension is £155.65 per week. However:

- Your National Insurance record is used to work out how much you will actually get.
- You usually need at least 10 qualifying years before you are entitled to any new State Pension.

Private pensions

There are a number of attractions in saving for your retirement through a private pension plan. If you are self-employed you will need to make your own arrangements. For those of you working in employment it is more than likely that your employer is running a scheme for the employees of the business that you can join.

Tax Saver

The main features of pension provision are:

- you receive full tax relief on your allowable premiums;
- your contributions are invested in a tax-free fund;
- you can take your benefits from the age of 55; and
- you do not have to retire to access your benefits.

(a) Annual contributions

You can get tax relief on the payment of pension contributions:

- up to 100 per cent of your annual earnings; but
- subject to a maximum annual allowance, which is £40,000.

However, for 2015/16 there are two 'notional pension input periods' from:

- 6 April 2015 to 8 July 2015; and
- 9 July 2015 to 5 April 2016.

In the first period you can contribute as much as £80,000 into your pension.

There is no allowance in the second period but you can carry forward from the first period to 8 July 2015 any of the unused allowance up to a maximum of £40,000.

The annual allowance:

- does not set a limit on pension contributions in a tax year; but
- is by reference to the 'pension input period' for each pension scheme ending in a tax year.

In calculating how much has been contributed you need to take into account:

- payments into all your pension schemes ending in the tax year; and
- any employer contributions.

If more than the annual allowance is contributed, the excess is taxed at your marginal rate of tax.

(b) Unused allowances

If your contributions exceed the annual allowance in a tax year, you will not be liable to the excess charge providing you have sufficient unused allowances brought forward from the three previous years.

Contributions are first of all allocated to the annual allowance for the current year. Any excess can then be set against any unused allowances bought forward. Those of an earlier year are used first.

Warren Baker is employed as a senior manager on a salary of £80,000 per annum. He is a member of his employer's pension scheme, which has a pension input period running from each 1 April to the following 31 March. The company contributes 10 per cent of Warren's salary towards his pension. He pays in 6 per cent of his salary. The contributions each year from Warren and his employer total £12,800.

In June 2018 Warren is awarded a bonus of £150,000 by his employer for securing a valuable long-term contract for the company.

Warren decides to pay £80,000 from the bonus into his pension as a one-off extra contribution. Warren's pension input amount in 2018/19 of £92,800 (£80,000 + £12,800) exceeds his annual allowance by £52,800. However, he has unused annual allowances brought forward from previous years as follows:

	Unused allowances bought forward (£)	Utilized in 2018/19 (£)	Carried forward (£)
2017/18	27,200	–	27,200
2016/17	27,200	22,400	4,800
2015/16	30,400	30,400	–
		52,800	

First of all Warren uses up all his unused allowances from the two pension input periods in 2015/16. This is followed by £22,400 from 2016/17 leaving unused allowances from 2016/17 and 2017/18 totalling £32,000 to carry forward to 2019/20.

(c) Drawing your pension from age 55

> **Tax Saver**
>
> Anyone with pension savings in what is known as a defined contribution scheme can take 25 per cent of the value of their fund tax free.

Until you dip into your pension fund it is called an uncrystallized fund. 25 per cent of any lump sums taken out of the fund are tax free; the balance is taxed as income. But once you start taking a regular income by:

- going into a regular drawdown plan; or
- purchasing an annuity,

only the first withdrawal of 25 per cent, or less, of the full value is free of tax.

However tempting it may be to withdraw a large chunk of money in one tax year from your pension savings you need to be aware that you could incur a very substantial tax bill.

In 2015/16 John Hill has a taxable income of £25,000. His tax bill, all at 20 per cent, is £2,880. His pension pot is £200,000 and he decides to take half of it. 25 per cent of the £100,000 withdrawal is tax free leaving £75,000 taxable. His tax liability for 2015/16 increases to £29,387.00 as follows:

	£
Taxable pension fund withdrawal	75,000
Other income	25,000
	100,000
Less: Personal allowance	10,600
Taxable income	£89,400
Income Tax payable	
£31,865 @ 20 per cent	6,373.00
£57,535 @ 40 per cent	23,014.00
	£29,387.00

Just over 75 per cent of the taxable part of the withdrawal bears tax at 40 per cent. If John had encased the entire fund:

- he would have lost his personal allowance of £10,600; and
- some of the pension pot would suffer tax at 45 per cent.

However, once you start drawing taxable income from your pension fund you are restricted to annual pension contributions of no more than £10,000.

Tax at source under the PAYE system is taken off by your pension provider on both:

- lump sum payments; and
- regular income,

drawn from your pension pot.

As it is more than likely that too much tax will be deducted from lump sum withdrawals, HMRC have introduced three new forms to reclaim any tax overpayment. These are:

- Form P50Z, which is used if you have cashed in your entire pension fund and you have no other income in the year;
- Form P53Z, which is relevant if you have withdrawn all your pension pot but you do have other taxable income in the year; and
- Form P55, which applies when you make a partial withdrawal but no further cash withdrawals are intended in the same tax year.

Savers who are thinking about taking money from their pension funds can access free guidance so they can better understand their retirement income options under these rules. This is available from either the Pensions Advisory Service or Citizens Advice.

(d) Small pension pots

If the amount of your pension savings is:

- less than £30,000 you can take it all in cash; or
- no more than £10,000 in each of three pension pots you can do the same.

However, remember that only 25 per cent of any lump sum is tax free.

(e) Lifetime allowance

There is a single lifetime allowance of £1.25m on the amount of your pension savings you can build up during your life that can benefit from tax relief. If the value of your pension fund is more than the lifetime allowance when you come to draw your pension you will be subject to tax on the excess, as follows:

- at 55 per cent if paid as a lump sum; or
- at 25 per cent on a taxable pension.

(f) Fixed protection

There are two ways you can protect pension rights built up from the lifetime allowance tax charge.

This is another aspect of your tax and financial affairs on which you should seek specialist advice.

(g) Death benefits

On death, special rules apply to funds held in a pension pot because Inheritance Tax (see Chapter 17) is not usually charged on money held in a pension.

Tax Saver

If you die before age 75 and leave funds in a defined contribution pension fund your nominated beneficiaries can inherit the fund tax free. This applies whether they:

- take one or more lump sum withdrawals; or
- use the fund for income.

But if you are over 75 years old when you die, a beneficiary who opts for:

- a lump sum will incur a tax charge of 45 per cent;
- regular amounts will pay Income Tax at his or her marginal rate on the income payments.

Kevin Arnold and his wife, Stella, have two children, Evan and Ella. Kevin has a defined contribution pension fund amounting to £560,000. He nominates Stella as the beneficiary of the fund in the event of his death. Kevin dies at age 74. Stella opts not to encash the fund tax free. Instead she withdraws a regular income which is not taxable.

Stella then nominates her two children as equal beneficiaries of the remaining fund. Stella dies at age 78. As she is over age 75 on her death, Evan and Ella will pay income tax at their respective marginal rates on whatever they withdraw from the fund.

Stakeholder pensions

Tax Saver

Even if you are not:

- earning; or

- paying tax,

you can contribute up to £3,600 per annum into a pension scheme and obtain tax relief at the basic rate.

You can set up a scheme for your spouse and each child or grandchild. As much as £2,880 can be invested every year into each separate pension plan. The remaining £720 is contributed by HMRC.

Savings and investment income

There are likely to be occasions during your lifetime when you will either be:

- making regular savings out of income;
- investing a lump sum from a pension scheme on retirement; or
- in receipt of a much more substantial sum such as an inheritance or, perhaps, winnings on the National Lottery.

Examples of savings and investment income are:

- bank or building society interest;
- share and unit trust dividends;
- rents;
- interest on government stocks; and
- income from a trust fund.

Tax-free income

Tax Saver

The most widely known investments where the return is tax free are some of those available from National Savings and Investments. Individuals in the top tax brackets should take a look at them. They are:

- Fixed-Interest and Index-Linked Savings Certificates*; and
- Premium Bond Prizes.

* although no issues are on general sale at the time of writing, the total value of any maturing certificates can be renewed.

Also tax free are:

- interest on cash ISAs;

- dividends from ISA investments; and

- dividends paid on shares in Venture Capital Trusts.

Tax-free income does not need to be reported on your annual Income Tax Return.

Interest and dividends

You will receive dividends on your shares or interest on your bank/building society accounts or British government stocks either:

- with a 10 per cent tax credit that cannot be reclaimed;

- less Income Tax at 20 per cent; or

- with no deduction for tax.

Non-repayable 10 per cent tax credit	Tax deducted at 20 per cent	No tax deducted

• Dividends on shares and unit trust holdings	• Bank and building society interest
	• National Savings Guaranteed Growth and Income Bonds
	• National Savings over aged 65 Bonds
	• Interest on fixed interest funds
	• Income element of purchased life annuities
		• National Savings:
		  – Direct Saver Account
		  – Investment Account
		  – Income Bonds
		• Interest on British Government Stocks
		• Tax Deposit Certificates
		• Single Deposits over £50,000 for a fixed period of less than five years*
		• Deposits with non-UK branches of banks and building societies

* only on deposits made before 6 April 2012.

You can, if you want, choose to receive the interest on holdings of British government stocks with tax deducted. To do so you will have to write to Computershare Investor Services to request this change.

In working out how much tax you have to pay each year, dividend and interest income is always regarded as the top part of your income. If you have both dividend and interest (savings) income, your dividends will be treated as the highest part. As a result:

- Non-taxpayers can only claim for a repayment of Income Tax on savings income where tax at 20 per cent has been deducted before payment. The 10 per cent tax credit on their dividend income is non-repayable.

Tanya Bridge, who is married to Derek, receives total investment income of £4,500 during 2015/16. £3,420 is the interest on her various building society accounts – £4,275 gross with tax of £855 (20 per cent) taken off at source – and dividends of £1,080 (£1,200 gross less a 10 per cent tax credit of £120).

Tanya's total income is less than her personal allowance of £10,600 but she can only claim back from HMRC the tax of £855 suffered on her interest income.

- Individuals able to benefit from the 0 per cent starting rate on savings income are able to reclaim all or some of the tax at 20 per cent deducted at source on this income.

Tanya's sister, Henrietta, earns £14,000 from part-time employment during 2015/16. All her savings are invested in cash deposits where she receives the interest with tax deducted and during the year it amounts to £2,000. Her tax repayment for the year is £320.00 as follows:

	Gross income (£)	Tax suffered (£)
Employment earnings	14,000	680.00
Interest income	2,500	500.00
	16,500	1,180.00
Less: Personal allowance	10,600	
Taxable income	£5,900	
Tax thereon: £4,300 @ 20 per cent		860.00
Repayment for 2014/15		£320.00

The income of £4,300 taxable at 20 per cent comprises:

- Tanya's earnings of £14,000 less her personal allowance of £10,600; and
- interest income of £900.

The nil rate band on savings income is reduced from £5,000 to £1,600 by the excess of Tanya's earnings over her personal allowance.

- Taxpayers liable at the basic rate of 20 per cent, but at neither the higher nor additional rates, do not pay any further tax on their dividend and interest income.

Tanya's aunt, Davina, receives building society interest, including tax deducted at source, of £400 in 2015/16. Her earned income, after allowances and reliefs, comes to £10,000. She pays tax for the year as follows:

on her earned income of   £10,000 @ 20 per cent
on her interest income of   £400 @ 20 per cent

- Individuals whose income takes them into the higher rate of 40 per cent must pay Income Tax of a further 20 per cent on their non-dividend savings income above the basic-rate band. If the income beyond the basic-rate band comes from dividends the extra tax payable is at 22.5 per cent on the total of dividends and their tax credits.

Tanya's husband, Derek, banks interest and dividend income amounting to £2,000 (gross) and £2,600 (including the 10 per cent tax credit) respectively during 2015/16. His earnings, after allowances and reliefs, total £30,000. His tax charge is worked out as follows:

on his earned income of	£30,000 @ 20 per cent
on his interest income of	£1,785 @ 20 per cent
on his interest income of	£215 @ 40 per cent
on his dividends of	£2,600 @ 32.5 per cent

The £1,785 slice of interest income attracts tax at the rate of 20 per cent as it falls within the limit of income of £31,785 taxed at the basic rate.

Tax Saver

Individuals not liable to tax can arrange to receive their interest gross. This is done by completing a special form (R85) that is available at banks, building societies, post offices and tax offices throughout the country as well as from the HMRC website. This will save them having to claim a refund from HMRC.

Accrued income

Interest on fixed-rate investments is regarded as accruing from day to day between payment dates. On a sale the vendor is charged Income Tax on the interest that has accrued from the previous payment date to the date of sale. The purchaser is allowed to deduct this amount from the interest received on the following payment date.

These arrangements cover both fixed and variable-rate stocks and bonds, including those issued by governments, companies and local authorities. But the arrangements will not affect you if the nominal value of your securities is under £5,000.

The interest on a holding of 6 per cent Treasury Stock 2028 is payable on each 7 June and 7 December. The half-yearly interest on a holding of £30,000, sold for settlement on 14 August 2015, is £900.

$$\text{Accrued proportion} = \frac{68 \times £900}{183} = £334.42$$

Rents

The letting of property, including isolated or casual lettings, is treated as a business for tax purposes. This applies to any flat, house, shop or other property that you rent to tenants. Most of the rules for working out the taxable profits from a trade or profession are also relevant in working out your annual income from the letting of property. Income from all your properties in the United Kingdom is pooled together, regardless of the type of lease. Also it does not matter whether the property is let furnished or unfurnished.

However, unlike a trade or profession, losses from your property rental business can only be carried forward to be set against future profits from the same activities.

Other than expenditure of a capital nature, such as that on extensions, structural alterations or improvements, the general running costs of a property can be set against rental income. Included in allowable expenses are:

- fees incurred on letting out the property, including estate agents' costs and those for drawing up the tenancy agreement and an inventory;
- rent collection and management costs;
- interest relating to your property letting business (it does not matter whether the interest is payable on a loan or overdraft);
- maintenance, repairs and redecorations;
- insurance premiums on buildings and contents policies;
- ground rent for leased premises;
- water rates and Council Tax;
- gardening, cleaning and security services;
- all other expenses of managing the property such as stationery, postage, advertising for tenants, etc; and
- your share of expenditure on the common parts of the let property.

Karen Donnelly owns a flat that she let out to tenants during 2015/16. The net rental income for the year amounts to £14,740 as follows:

	£	£
Rent receivable from the flat		21,000
Less: Expenses		
Agents fees for letting	2,467	
Management fees	740	
Ground rent	200	
Service charges	1,103	
Council tax for tenants	960	
Water rates	220	
Lounge redecoration	490	
Boiler repair	80	
		6,260
2015/16 net rental income		£14,740

Tax Saver

Expenditure you incur, such as that on advertising or repairs, prior to a letting can be deducted from the rents you receive in the first year so long as the costs:

- are incurred within seven years prior to the commencement of the letting business; and
- would have been tax allowable if incurred once the business had started.

Where you are renting out:

- Unfurnished property: you can claim capital allowances on the cost of fixtures, fittings and equipment spent on the let property.
- Furnished property: you are allowed an additional deduction to cover the cost of wear and tear to furnishings and fittings. A 'furnished property' is defined as: 'one which is capable of normal occupation without the tenant having to provide their own beds, chairs, tables, sofas and other furnishings, cooker etc.'

You can either deduct:

- what you actually spend on renewing your furnishings and fittings; or
- a fixed allowance equivalent to 10 per cent of the rent you receive less amounts paid out on Council Tax and water rates.

If Karen's flat in the preceding illustration had been let furnished, this allowance would amount to £1,982 as follows:

	£
Rent receivable	21,000
Less: Council Tax and water rates	1,180
	19,820
Wear and tear allowance: 10 per cent	£1,982

Tax Saver

If you are contemplating the purchase of a property that you are then going to let out as an investment, it may well pay you to take out a loan to assist in financing the purchase. You will be able to claim the annual interest on the borrowing as a deduction from the net rental income of the property.

Tax Saver

Alternatively remortgage your buy-to-let property, releasing funds for other uses and still get tax relief on the interest.

Rent-a-room

Income from the furnished letting of spare rooms in your home as residential accommodation is tax free providing the gross rents do not exceed £4,250 per annum. The space you let out must be in your only or main home, which can be a house, flat, caravan or even a houseboat.

You can elect to opt out of this special form of relief. It will pay you to make the opt-out election if, for example, there is a loss on the letting that can be set against your other rental profits under the normal rules dealing with income from lettings.

Where your annual gross rents are more than £4,250 you must elect if you want to pay tax on the excess gross rents, without any relief for expenses. If you do not do so then you will have to work out your taxable income using the rules for lettings income.

Theresa Stevens is a basic-rate taxpayer who lets out a room in her bungalow to a lodger paying £110 per week, £5,720 for 2015/16. The expenses that could be set against the lodger's rents total £1,600 for the year.

Theresa elects for rent-a-room relief and her Income Tax liability is £294.00 (£5,720 – £4,250) x 20 per cent. Under the normal rules her tax liability would come to £824.00 (£5,720 – £1,600) x 20 per cent.

The tax-free limit of £4,250 is halved where an individual and some other person are each entitled to income under the scheme. Each lessor's exempt amount is then £2,125.

Tax Saver

If you need more income and do not want to move home, why not rent out a room to a lodger or bed-and-breakfast guest? Up to £4,250 a year (equivalent to a weekly rent of £81.70) is tax free under this type of relief.

Non-qualifying life policies

At the outset, a lump sum premium is paid into a bond that is, for example, either investment based or intended to produce a guaranteed income. An investor can usually:

- take regular amounts out;

- make ad hoc partial withdrawals; or

- leave the bond untouched until encashment or death, when it will form part of the investor's estate.

There is no tax relief on the single premium. Neither Capital Gains Tax nor Income Tax at the savings rate is payable on any profit. But investors whose income takes them into either the higher or additional rates of 40 per cent or 45 per cent will pay tax at the difference between their top rate and the basic rate of Income Tax on chargeable events. These arise on:

- surrender or maturity of the policy;

- death of the life assured; or

- withdrawals in excess of a cumulative allowance built up at the time.

At the end of each policy year an allowance of 5 per cent of the original investment is given. This can be carried forward from year to year. Over a period of 20 years, allowances of up to 100 per cent of the initial investment will be given. A taxable gain only arises if the amount of the withdrawal is more than the cumulative allowance at the time. Then it is the excess that is taxed.

Edward Clark invests £15,000 in an investment bond. Withdrawals of £600, £900 and £3,250 are made during the second, third and fifth policy years. The annual allowance is £750, being 5 per cent, of the original investment. A taxable gain of £1,000 arises in year five as follows:

Number of policy years	Cumulative allowance (£)	Amount withdrawn (£)	Cumulative withdrawals (£)	Taxable amount (£)
1	750	–	–	–
2	1,500	600	600	–
3	2,250	900	1,500	–
4	3,000	–	1,500	–
5	3,750	3,250	4,750	1,000

When the final chargeable event on a bond occurs, the taxable gain is calculated by taking into account all previous withdrawals and taxable gains.

After seven years, Edward encashes the investment bond in the illustration above for £21,050. The taxable gain amounts to £9,800 as follows:

	£	£
Policy proceeds		21,050
Add: Withdrawals in years 2, 3 and 5		4,750
		25,800
Less: Original investment	15,000	
Amount already taxed	1,000	
		16,000
Taxable gain on encashment		£9,800

The method of calculating the Income Tax due on the taxable gain involves a number of stages, including 'top slicing' relief.

Edward is a single man. During 2015/16 his other income, all earnings, amounted to £42,000. He pays tax of £1,421.00 on the gain of £9,800 on the final encashment of his bond worked out as follows:

Gain on encashment of bond	£9,800
Number of years held	7
Taxable slice of gain	£1,400
Taxable income – excluding slice of gain	
Earnings	£42,000
Less: Personal allowance	£10,600
	£31,400
Tax applicable to slice of gain	
On first £385 (£31,785 – £31,400) @ 0 per cent	–
On next £1,015 (excess over £31,785) @ 20 per cent (40 per cent – 20 per cent)	£203.00
Average rate on slice	14.5%
The tax payable on the gain = £9,800 @ 14.5 per cent =	£1,421.00

Tax Saver

A non-qualifying life policy such as a single premium investment bond is:

- a good way to supplement your income; and
- particularly for anyone in the top tax brackets.

Individual Savings Account

An Individual Savings Account (ISA) can include:

- cash (including National Savings); or
- stocks and shares.

Tax Saver

You do not pay any tax on the interest you earn in a cash ISA. Also free of tax are the income or capital profits in a stocks and shares ISA.

You can subscribe to an ISA if you are:

- both resident and ordinarily resident in the United Kingdom for tax purposes; and
- aged 18 or over, although 16- and 17-year-olds can invest just in cash.

Tax Saver

The annual subscription limit for all qualifying individuals:

- is £15,240 in cash;
- can be saved in just one type of account or split between both kinds; and
- is increased each year in line with the Retail Prices Index rounded to a convenient multiple of £120 to allow for the easy calculation of monthly contributions.

In May 2015 Lance Bishop put cash of £9,000 into a stocks and shares ISA. This left him with up to £6,240 available to invest in either a cash ISA or his stocks and shares ISA during the rest of 2015/16.

From the autumn of 2015 it has been possible for you to make withdrawals and then replace money in your cash ISA within the same tax year without these transactions counting towards your annual subscription limit.

> ### Tax Saver
>
> Spouses and civil partners can make an additional contribution to their ISAs equivalent to the value of their deceased spouses or partners ISAs at the date of death.

Other features of an ISA are:

- there is no statutory lock-in period or minimum subscription;
- you can make withdrawals whenever you like; and
- there is no lifetime investment limit.

The list of investments that qualify for the stocks and shares component include:

- shares listed on a recognized Stock Exchange;
- shares quoted on the Alternative Investment Market;
- Unit Trusts;
- Investment Trusts;
- open-ended investment companies (OEIC); and
- government stocks with at least five years to go to maturity.

Help-to-Buy ISA

This tax-free savings scheme is a must for anyone aged 16 or over saving for a deposit on their first home. It is available from various banks and building societies for four years from the start of December 2015. The key features of these new accounts for first time buyers are:

- they are limited to one for each individual, rather than one per home – so those buying together can each open an account;
- you can save up to £1,200 in the first month. In each subsequent month this limit is £200. But you cannot save through both Help-to-Buy and cash ISAs in the same tax years.

Tax Saver

The Government contributes 25 per cent tax free to your savings at the time you use it for a deposit on your first home. You need to save at least £1,600 to qualify for the minimum bonus. The maximum bonus is £3,000 on savings of £12,000.

The bonus is only paid when you buy your first home in the UK. It is only available on purchases of up to £250,000 outside London and £450,000 in London.

Should you subsequently decide not to buy a house the account will still be tax free. However, you will not qualify for the Government bonus.

Enterprise Investment Scheme

The aims of the scheme are twofold:

- to provide a targeted incentive for equity investment in unquoted trading companies, which helps overcome the problems faced by such companies in raising modest amounts of equity finance; and

- to encourage outside investors previously unconnected with the company, who introduce finance and expertise, by allowing them actively to participate in the management of the company as paid directors without losing entitlement to relief.

The main features of the scheme are:

- Income Tax relief at 30 per cent on qualifying investments up to £1 million in a tax year.
- Subject to the annual £1 million subscription limit, the Income Tax relief can be carried back to the previous year.
- All shares in a qualifying company must be held for at least three years, otherwise the Income Tax relief will be clawed back.
- Losses made on the disposal of qualifying shares are eligible for relief from either Income Tax or Capital Gains Tax.

Seed Enterprise Investment Scheme

This scheme:

- runs alongside the Enterprise Investment Scheme; but
- is targeted at smaller companies in the early stage of their development.

The main features of this scheme are:

- Income Tax Relief at 50 per cent on qualifying investments up to £100,000 in a tax year.
- The 50 per cent rate of relief does not depend on the investor's top personal tax rate; it is calculated on the amount invested and given as a credit against the investor's total tax liability.
- The Income Tax relief can be carried back to the previous year.
- All shares in a qualifying company must be held for at least three years; otherwise the Income Tax relief will be clawed back.

Venture Capital Trusts

Venture Capital Trusts (VCTs) are a type of Investment Trust with tax advantages designed to encourage investment in the under-nourished small business sector. Individuals investing in VCTs are eligible for the following Income Tax incentives:

- Relief at 30 per cent on subscriptions for new ordinary shares up to £200,000 in any tax year, providing the shares are held for at least five years.
- Tax-free dividends.

The 30 per cent income tax relief is deductible from the total income tax payable and does not depend on the investing individual's marginal tax rate.

Overseas investment income

Generally, income from investments or savings abroad is taxed in the same way as your onshore dividends or interest income. Foreign tax paid, subject to certain restrictions, can be offset against the tax payable here on the same income. If required, you must be able to show that you have actually paid, or suffered, the overseas tax.

Joint income

Income from assets such as bank/building society accounts, property or shares held in the joint names of a married couple or civil partners is treated for tax purposes as belonging to them in equal proportions. If the actual proportions of ownership between the couple are unequal, they can make an election for the income on any jointly owned assets to be taxed in accordance with their respective entitlements to the income. There is a special form to complete. The declaration applies from the date it is made.

But dividends from jointly owned shares in a small family company are taxed on husband and wife according to their actual ownership, rather than in equal shares.

Tax Saver

Income splitting is likely to be of relevance to some taxpayers as a means of reducing their overall tax burden in view of:

- the restriction to the personal allowance for individuals with incomes of more than £100,000; and

- the 45 per cent rate of Income Tax on incomes in excess of £150,000.

The family unit

11

Gone are the days when it was commonplace for couples to marry. Many now prefer to live together as partners. Opposite-sex couples may even have children without marrying, or marry later on in life.

Living together

There are no special tax breaks for couples living with one another as partners. They are each taxed as single people. Furthermore, it is mandatory that income from jointly owned assets must be split between them in accordance with the ratio of their respective interests in such assets. Assets cannot be transferred between them without avoiding a possible liability to Capital Gains Tax at the time of transfer.

Marriage

Husband and wife:

- are taxed separately on their income and capital gains;
- are each entitled to personal allowances that can be set against their own income, whether from earnings or investments;
- can each have taxable income, after allowances and reliefs of £31,785 for 2015/16 before either of them is liable to tax at the higher rate of 40 per cent (they may, of course, need to rearrange their affairs to take maximum advantage of potential tax savings; in contrast to the position of unmarried couples this is easily done);
- must complete their own Tax Returns every year; and
- are each responsible for settling their respective tax liabilities.

These rules also apply to same-sex couples who have legalized their relationship by forming a Civil Partnership.

Children

Tax Saver

A child or teenager is:

- treated as an individual for tax purposes like anyone else;
- entitled to the personal allowance – £10,600 for 2015/16 – so no tax is payable on any earnings or other income up to this limit;
- also a taxable person for the purposes of Capital Gains Tax (Chapter 13) and Inheritance Tax (Chapter 17).

But, the income from a gift by a parent in favour of an unmarried minor child is regarded as the parents' income for tax purposes – subject to an annual £100 limit for small amounts of income.

Tax Saver

Grandparents or other relatives can, however:

- give savings to their grandchildren, nieces, nephews, etc, without the same restrictions applying to the taxation of income on any such gifts; or
- with the benefit of professional advice, set up a discretionary settlement with grandchildren among the class of beneficiaries. Such trusts suffer tax at 45 per cent on their income. As a result, taking the personal allowance into account, all or some of the tax suffered by the trustees on the income paid out for the benefit of a minor beneficiary should be repayable.

A few years ago Jeremy Chandler created a discretionary trust. In 2015/16 the trustees resolved to distribute income of £2,000 for the benefit of his young granddaughter, Veronica. This is her only income in the year. Her parents can recover Income Tax of £1,636 for Veronica as follows:

	Income (£)	Tax (£)
Trust distribution	3,636	1,636.00
Less: Personal allowance	10,600	
Taxable income	Nil	
Repayment for 2015/16		£1,636.00

Parents, civil partners or those responsible for children do not get a general tax allowance for their children. However:

- You should be able to claim Child Benefit. It does not depend on income.
- If you are on a low or modest income, you should be able to claim the Child Tax Credit.
- Depending on your personal circumstances you may be entitled to one or more of the numerous other Social Security benefits associated with children.

It is down to parents or guardians to complete and sign Tax Returns or Repayment Claims for their children up to age 18.

High Income Child Benefit charge

This is a charge on a taxpayer:

- who has net income of more than £50,000 in a tax year; and
- either they, or their wife/partner is receiving Child Benefit.

Where both spouses or partners have net incomes exceeding £50,000, the charge is paid by the spouse or partner with the higher income.

The tax liability:

- is charged at 1 per cent for each £100 of net income between £50,000 and £60,000; and
- is equal to the amount of child benefit where net income exceeds £60,000.

Claimants of Child Benefit can opt not to receive the benefit if they or their spouse/partner want to avoid paying the charge.

Tax Saver

Electing not to receive Child Benefit is not the same as not making a claim in the first instance. A claim should always be made then should be followed by the opt out. This ensures the claimant, usually the mother, is credited with National Insurance Contributions. As a result entitlement to the State Pension or other benefits is not jeopardized.

Joel Haynes and his wife, Cleo, have two children. Joel's adjusted net income for 2015/16 is £58,500. Cleo received Child Benefit totalling £1,788.80 for the year (£20.70 each week for the elder child plus £13.70 a week for the younger child = £34.40 x 52 weeks = £1,788.80). Joel's High Income Child Benefit Charge for 2015/16 is £1,511.98 = 85% (£58,500 − £50,000 ÷ 100) x £1,778.80.

The Child Trust Fund

The Child Trust Fund (CTF) is a savings and investment plan for children born before 1 January 2011.

The main features of continuing accounts which existed then are:

- Up to £4,080 in total can be added to the fund each year by family and friends.
- All income and capital growth within a CTF is tax free.
- It can be accessed at age 18.

There are a wide range of organizations offering CTF accounts linked to either cash deposits, unit trusts or even equities.

It is now possible for parents with Child Tax Funds to get a better deal by transferring the funds to Junior Individual Savings Accounts.

Junior Individual Savings Account

Any child resident in the United Kingdom, under the age of 18, and who does not have a Child Trust Fund account, is eligible for a Junior Individual Savings Account (JISA).

A JISA is a tax efficient way to save for your child's future. The main features of a JISA are:

- The account can be opened and managed by the person with parental responsibility for the child.

- Up to a fixed amount can be invested each year.

- The annual investment limit for 2015/16 is £4,080.

- All returns are tax free.

Other features of a JISA are:

- family or friends can also contribute up to the amount of the annual allowance;

- the funds in a JISA can be invested in cash or stocks and shares; and

- it can be accessed by the child at age 18.

Separation and divorce

Not only does the breakdown of a marriage cause much personal suffering but it invariably has consequences for tax purposes.

A married couple are no longer considered to be living together when:

- they are separated by a Deed or Court Order; or

- they are living apart in such a way that permanent separation is inevitable.

If a married couple are entitled to the married couple's allowance, the full allowance can be claimed by the husband for the tax year in which the marriage fails, but if he remarries in the same year he cannot also claim that part of the allowance due for the period following the wedding.

Maintenance payments are tax free in the hands of the recipient, but only limited tax relief is available to the payer of maintenance under a Court Order, Child Support Agency assessment or written agreement as follows:

- Either the payer or recipient must be born before 6 April 1935.
- The payment must be to the divorced or separated spouse.
- The maximum amount of tax relief to which the payer is entitled in 2015/16 is 10 per cent of the lesser of £3,220 or the actual maintenance paid each year.
- No tax relief can be claimed on maintenance paid to, or for the benefit of, children of the marriage.

The tax implications for civil partners who separate are no different to those for a married couple. Similarly the dissolution of a Civil Partnership has the same consequences as a divorce of an opposite-sex couple.

Old age

When it comes to tax, getting older does not mean an easier life. Pensioners have to deal with the tax system in the same way as everyone else. Nevertheless, there are some factors that are only relevant to:

- the finances of elderly persons; and
- working out how much tax they must pay each year.

First and foremost come the age allowances. In Chapter 2, I explained how an older taxpayer calculates the amount of these allowances to which he or she is entitled. Of particular significance:

Tax Saver

are the rules allowing elderly couples to transfer the married couple's allowance between them. This can sometimes save on tax.

Tax Saver

is the income limit for the married couple's allowance, which is by reference to the husband's income or that of the spouse/civil partner with a higher income as the case may be. These rules apply even if entitlement to this allowance arises because of the age of the other spouse/civil partner.

Men qualify to receive the State Pension when they reach age 65; for women this date depends on when they were born between 6 April 1950 and 5 April 1955.

On reaching retirement age a pensioner has three options:

- retire and claim the state pension;
- carry on working and claim the state pension; or
- put off claiming the state pension.

All pensions, including a State Pension, are taxable. There is, however, no mechanism to deduct any Income Tax at source from payment of the State Pension. Therefore, in addition to including a pensioner's personal allowance in the coding notice of an occupational or personal pension taxed under PAYE, a deduction from allowances equivalent to the annual amount of the State Pension is also incorporated. In this way:

- the tax due on the State Pension is collected; and
- the need to make a direct tax payment is avoided.

The significance of the following letters at the end of a Code Number is as follows:

- L – for people born after 5 April 1938 and due the basic personal allowance.
- Y – means you are due the higher personal allowance as you were born before 6 April 1938.
- T – applies in most other circumstances.

If a pensioner's State Pension and other deductions exceeds his or her personal allowance, HMRC issue a 'K' Coding. The amount of the negative allowance is then added to the pension on which tax is paid.

Taxpayers approaching State Pension age should make sure that their Notice of Coding is changed to include an estimate of the amount of their State Pension for the year. Usually HMRC sends such taxpayers a Form P161 asking for details about pension entitlement. This information is then used to amend tax codes as appropriate.

Nowadays many people carry on working after they retire from their main job or self-employment. They may decide to make use of all the knowledge and experience built up during their working lives by setting up in business as a consultant, or take a part-time position in, for example, a retail outlet.

Owen Wilcox is single and 69. During 2015/16 he received a State Pension of £112.25 per week and an annual pension from his previous employer of £8,000. To keep himself occupied he worked part-time at his local DIY store, earning a weekly wage of £105 for 46 weeks of the year. Owen paid Income Tax for 2015/16 of £1,613.40 as follows:

	Income (£)	Tax (£)
State Pension	5,837	–
Occupational Pension	8,000	647.40
Wages	4,830	966.00
	18,667	1,613.40
Less: Personal Allowance	10,600	
Taxable Income	£8,067	
Income Tax payable		
£8,067 @ 20 per cent		£1,613.40

The tax code used for working out the Income Tax to be deducted from Owen's occupational pension is 476L. This is based on the difference between Owen's personal allowance of £10,600 and his State Pension of £5,837. Tax at the basic rate of 20 per cent, under a BR Code, would have been deducted from Owen's wage from the DIY store.

Tax Saver

Elderly couples, in particular, need to pay great care and attention to their respective incomes. They should make sure that their investments and savings are arranged such that they do not lose out on either:

- any personal age allowance which is due; and/or
- the married couple's allowance only for tax payers born before 6 April 1935.

They should also remain mindful of the annual income limit above which allowances are restricted. It may pay couples on modest incomes to transfer capital between them.

Alternatively, it may pay them to shift some of their savings income into tax-free investments such as National Savings or ISAs. In either case, by doing so, they may avoid losing some of their age-related allowances.

Bert and Mavis Wilkins, a married couple, both in their late 80s, whose joint income for 2015/16 amounted to £54,500, paid Income Tax totalling £6,237.00 on this sum. This all related to Bert's income as follows:

	Bert (£)	Mavis (£)
State Pensions	6,029	3,614
Occupational Pensions	18,971	6,796
Building Society interest gross equivalent	12,890	–
Interest on British government stocks	5,000	1,200
	42,890	11,610
Less: Personal Allowance	10,600	10,660
Taxable Income	32,290	950
Income Tax Payable		
£ – / £950 @ 0 per cent	–	–
£31,785 / – @ 20 per cent	6,357.00	–
£505 / – @ 40 per cent	202.00	–
	6,559.00	–
Less: Relief for married couple's allowance – £3,220 @ 10 per cent	322.00	–
	£6,237.00	–

Bert's income is above the upper limit for entitlement to either the personal age or married couple's allowances.

Significant tax savings of £436.50 for 2015/16 could have been achieved by the couple if Bert had transferred capital to Mavis as follows:

	Bert (£)	Mavis (£)
State Pensions	6,029	3,614
Occupational Pensions	18,971	6,796
Building society interest gross equivalent	1,100	11,790
Interest on British government stocks	900	5,300
	27,000	27,500
Less: Personal Allowance	10,660	10,660
Taxable income	16,340	16,840
Income Tax payable		
£16,340 / £16,840 @ 20 per cent	3,268.00	3,368.00
	3,268.00	3,368.00
Less: Relief for married couple's allowance – £8,355 @ 10 per cent	835.50	–
	£2,432.50	£3,368.00

Death

Sadly, death comes to all of us and has tax consequences for married couples, which are as follows:

- The married couple's allowance is not restricted in the year of death of either spouse.

- Where the husband dies first, he is due his full personal allowance in the year of death. If he cannot use up the full married couple's allowance, because he has a low income, then the balance can be transferred to his widow.

- If the wife dies before her husband she will be due her full personal allowance in the year of death.

Civil partners are treated no differently.

Residence and domicile

12

As a general rule Income Tax is charged by the United Kingdom on:

- an individual's income arising in the United Kingdom irrespective of whether that person is resident here; and
- overseas income belonging to an individual resident in the United Kingdom.

Apart from some special cases, the amount of tax you pay each year depends on:

- whether you are resident in the United Kingdom; and
- in some circumstances on your domicile.

Not only are the two concepts of residence and domicile of fundamental importance in working out an individual's liability to UK taxation on income, but they are equally relevant for the purposes of both Capital Gains Tax and Inheritance Tax.

Residence

There are statutory rules to determine whether an individual is, or is not, a resident in the UK. Under the statutory residence test an individual is tax resident if either of the following are met, namely:

- automatic residence test; or
- the sufficient ties test which determines residence status based on a combination of days spent in, and various ties with, the UK.

The automatic residence test

If you can answer 'yes' to any one of the following overseas tests you are automatically not resident in the UK for that tax year.

- Did you spend less than 16 days in the UK?*
- Were you in the UK for less than 46 days and have you been not resident in the UK for all of the previous three tax years?
- Were you in full-time employment abroad and spent less than
  - 91 days in the UK; and
  - fewer than 31 of those days working in the UK?**

However, you are automatically UK resident for a tax year if you:

- are not automatically non-resident; and
- can reply 'yes' to any of these UK tests.

They are:

- Did you spend more than 182 days in the UK?
- Did you work full-time in the UK?
- Did you have a UK home in which you resided for more than 30 days, with no home abroad?***

*   this test does not apply if you die in the tax year. It is then replaced by other tests.
**   a day at work in the UK means that you spend at least three hours working in the UK on that day.
***   a home in the UK is any property which is available to you for at least 91 days in the tax year.

Sufficient ties test

This is an alternative test if you do not meet either the automatic overseas or UK residence tests.

Then, the UK residence for a tax year of either:

- an individual leaving the UK to go abroad (a 'leaver'); or
- a person coming to the UK from overseas (an 'arriver'),

depends on:

- how many days they spend in the UK; and
- how many of the following five connecting factors that they satisfy.

These are:

- Is your family UK resident?
- Do you have accommodation in the UK which is available to you?
- Have you spent at least 40 days working in the UK?
- Have you been in the UK for more than 90 days during either of the last two tax years?
- Have you spent more time in the UK than in any other country? ('leavers' only).

If you are:

- a 'leaver'; and
- have been UK resident in any one of the last three tax years,

your residence status is determined by the following table.

Days spent in the UK	Only resident if you satisfy
Less than 16	Always non-resident
16 to 45	Four or more connecting factors
46 to 90	Three or more connecting factors
91 to 120	Two or more connecting factors
121 to 182	One or more connecting factors
Over 182	Always resident

If you are:

- an 'arriver'; and
- have not been UK resident in any one of the last three tax years,

your residence status is governed by the following table:

Days spent in the UK	Only resident if you satisfy
Less than 16	Always non-resident
16 to 45	Always non-resident
46 to 90	Four or more connecting factors
91 to 120	Three or more connecting factors
121 to 182	Two or more connecting factors
Over 182	Always resident

Working abroad: expenses

Tax relief is allowed on the costs you incur on travel expenses in relation to your overseas employment. Nor will you be taxed on the following expenses borne by your employer:

- The cost of board and lodging outside the United Kingdom.
- Your travelling expenses, which also extends to unlimited return visits to the United Kingdom during longer assignments abroad.
- The travelling expenses of your spouse and children to visit you overseas. No more than two return visits by the same person are allowed each year and you must be working abroad for a continuous period of at least 60 days.

Leaving the United Kingdom permanently

Where you go abroad to live permanently, or are outside the United Kingdom for three years or more, you will cease to be UK resident from the day following your departure.

Tax Saver

Before you leave, ask your tax office for the special form (P85) relevant to individuals going abroad. You can use this form to claim tax relief or a tax refund for the year during which you leave the UK if you:

- worked or lived here;

- are leaving;

- may not come back; or

- are going to work abroad full-time for at least one full tax year.

The information on the form will also enable HMRC to consider your residence position.

As a non-resident you will not usually pay UK tax on:

- the State Pension; and
- interest on Government securities.

Allowances for non-UK residents

If you are not resident here but have taxable income in the United Kingdom, you may be able to reduce your tax bill by claiming UK tax allowances. These will generally be the same as those granted to an individual resident in the United Kingdom and can be claimed by the following individuals:

- a national of a state within the European Economic Area;
- a present or former employee of the British Crown;
- a resident of the Isle of Man or the Channel Islands;
- a widow or widower of a Crown Servant;
- a person employed by a missionary society; or
- a person abroad for health reasons following UK residence.

Non-resident Commonwealth citizens may be able to claim UK tax allowances under the Double Taxation Agreement concluded between the country where they are resident and the United Kingdom.

Income from UK property

Many individuals rent out their homes while they are living or working overseas. You can apply to HMRC for a certificate authorizing your tenant, or managing agent, to make payments of rent to you without withholding any UK tax. If you do not apply for a certificate or one is not issued to you, tax at the basic rate must be withheld from all remittances of rent to you by your managing agent or tenant.

Whether or not tax is deducted by your tenant or letting agent, while you are non-UK resident you are still liable to UK tax on income arising from the letting out of your property here.

However, you will not actually have to pay any UK tax if your income from property after allowable expenses, and any other taxable income, is less than any allowances that you may be entitled to claim.

Tax Saver

Non-resident married couples or civil partners with let property in the United Kingdom should consider putting their properties into joint ownership. It might then be possible for both parties to claim their personal allowance in working out the tax payable on their respective shares of the rental income.

Double taxation relief

If you move to a country with which the United Kingdom has concluded a Double Taxation Agreement, you may be able to claim partial or full exemption from UK tax on certain types of income such as:

- pensions and annuities; and
- royalties and dividends.

Furthermore, many Double Taxation Agreements contain clauses dealing with the special circumstances of:

- teachers and researchers;
- students and apprentices; and
- entertainers and sportsmen/women.

Going abroad: Capital Gains Tax

If:

- you have been resident in the United Kingdom for at least four out of the last seven years ending with the day before you leave; and
- within five complete years, you return here to take up residence for tax purposes again,

you will remain within the charge to Capital Gains Tax.

It follows that:

- gains realized in the tax year of departure will be taxed in that year; and
- all gains in subsequent years, including the year of return, will be subject to tax in the year when residence resumes.

However, profits made on assets bought and sold during the years of non-UK tax residence are tax free in the United Kingdom.

Albert Rogers, who had lived his whole life in the United Kingdom, accepted an offer to work abroad and left the United Kingdom on 27 March 2012. On 17 July 2013 he sold an investment, which he owned when he left the United Kingdom, realizing a profit of £25,000. He returned to the United Kingdom to take up residence again on 3 November 2015.

As Albert:

- had only been abroad for three complete tax years (2012/13, 2013/14, 2014/15); and
- was a resident in the United Kingdom for at least four of the seven tax years preceding his departure,

he will have to pay Capital Gains Tax on the gain of £25,000 in 2014/15.

Residential property in the United Kingdom

If:

- you are non-resident; and
- have sold or disposed of UK residential property,

you must tell HMRC within 30 days of conveyance.

You have to report the disposal within this time limit even if:

- the disposal results in a loss;
- there is no tax to pay; or
- you are already registered for Self Assessment.

Only that part of the gain relating to the period after 5 April 2015 is taxable. There are two ways of working this out. Either by:

- establishing the value of the property on 5 April 2015 and then calculating the gain based on this amount; or
- apportioning the gain equally over the total period of ownership.

The following chapter on capital gains sets out:

- the various reliefs; and
- the rates of tax,

for working out how much tax will be payable on the profit you made.

Coming to the United Kingdom permanently

Perhaps:

- you have been working overseas, your contract has finished and you have decided to return home; or
- you lived abroad and have now accepted a job offer in the United Kingdom.

You should:

- let HMRC know when you arrive in the United Kingdom; and
- apply for a National Insurance number (NINO) if you do not already have one and intend to work here.

You can claim the full UK personal allowance for the year of arrival. Where your job is with either a UK or an overseas employer and the duties of that employment will be performed wholly in the United Kingdom, the full amount of your salary will be taxable here.

Tax Saver

Before you leave the country where you have been living there may be opportunities to save on UK tax before taking up residence here. For example, it may pay you to close any bank or building society accounts before arrival as you would otherwise face the prospect of a charge to UK Income Tax on interest accrued, but not credited, while abroad.

Domicile

Domicile is a concept of general law. It is distinct from residence or nationality.

When you are born you acquire a domicile of origin from your father. Until you are 16 years old your domicile follows that of the person on whom you are legally dependent. At age 16 you have the option to abandon your existing domicile in favour of a domicile of choice. To do so you must sever all links and leave your current country or state and settle elsewhere. You will need to provide good evidence of your intention to live there indefinitely or permanently.

A wife's domicile is not necessarily the same as her husband's if they were married after the end of 1973. It is governed by the same factors as for any other individual with an independent domicile. However, a woman who married before the beginning of 1974 automatically acquired her husband's domicile on marriage. As long as the marriage lasts, her domicile only alters when there is any change in the domicile of her husband.

Taxation of non-domiciliaries

Adult non-UK domiciled taxpayers who are claiming to be taxed on remittances of income to the United Kingdom, and who claim non-UK domiciled status when claiming the remittance basis on their annual Self Assessment Tax Return:

- will lose their entitlement to the personal allowance on income and the annual exempt limit on capital gains; and

- will have to pay an annual charge in order to claim the remittance basis unless unremitted foreign income and gains are less than a *de minimis* limit of £2,000.

The annual charge:

- is £30,000 for an individual who has been resident for at least seven of the previous nine tax years;
- increases to £60,000 for an individual who has been resident for at least 12 of the previous 14 tax years;
- goes up to £90,000 for an individual who has been resident for at least 17 of the previous 20 tax years;
- is payable in addition to Income Tax due on income remitted to the United Kingdom; and
- is not itself taxed as a remittance if paid directly from an offshore source to HMRC.

Furthermore, the unremitted income or gains on which the tax charge is paid will not be taxed again if and when remitted to the United Kingdom.

Tax Saver

A non-domiciled taxpayer can, however, bring overseas income and gains into the United Kingdom free of tax for the purposes of making a commercial investment in a qualifying business.

Taxpayers who can claim the remittance basis do not have to do so. If they do not:

- they will then be taxed in the same way as other UK residents on income and gains arising in the tax year;
- tax will be payable on their worldwide income and gains for that tax year;
- they will be able to claim a personal allowance and the annual exempt limit on capital gains; and
- they will need to complete a Self Assessment Tax Return in order to report any foreign income and gains for that tax year.

Tax Saver

Individuals entitled to claim the remittance basis can decide from year to year whether they want to do so. In one year individuals:

- might choose to pay the annual £30,000, £60,000 or £90,000 charge and lose their allowances; and

- in the next year opt to pay tax on their worldwide income and gains on the arising basis.

This is certainly an issue on which I recommend you seek professional advice.

Capital gains

The profits you make on disposing of your assets are known as capital gains and are subject to Capital Gains Tax. However, not all capital receipts are taxable. These include lottery, pools or gambling winnings, mortgage cash-backs and personal or professional damages. Profits made on disposing of the following types of asset are also tax free:

- private cars;
- National Savings;
- your home;
- chattels sold for less than £6,000;
- British government securities and many corporate bonds;
- shares issued under either the Enterprise Investment or Seed Enterprise Investment Schemes as long as the income tax relief has not been withdrawn;
- shares in Venture Capital Trusts;
- shares issued under an employee shareholder agreement;
- investments in an Individual Savings Account (ISA);
- gifts to charities or for the public benefit; and
- qualifying life policies on your life.

Taxable gains

This list includes profits you realize from disposing of:

- property;
- shares and unit trust investments; or
- chattels sold for more than £6,000.

For Capital Gains Tax purposes, the date when the contract for purchase or sale is made determines the date when an asset is acquired or sold.

Tax payable

Every tax year you can make gains up to the annual exemption limit without paying tax. For 2015/16 the tax-free allowance is £11,100. Chargeable gains over and above this limit are taxed at flat rates of either 18 per cent or 28 per cent. This is because the rate at which you pay is found by adding the gains to your taxable income.

As a result:

- The 28 per cent rate will always apply if any part of your income bears tax above the basic rate.

- Tax at 18 per cent will be payable if both your income and gains above the annual exemption limit together do not exceed the basic rate limit: £31,785 for 2015/16.

- Where your gains when added to your income exceed the basic rate limit you will pay tax at:
  - 18 per cent on the amount of the gains within the basic rate band; and
  - 28 per cent on the excess.

Isaac Woolf realized gains of £18,000 during 2015/16. His taxable income, after personal allowances and reliefs, was £28,000. The Capital Gains Tax he owes for the year is £1,553.50 as follows:

	£
Realized gains	18,000
Less: Exemption limit	11,100
	6,900
Tax payable	
£3,785 @ 18 per cent	681.30
£3,115 @ 28 per cent	872.20
	£1,553.50

The amount of Capital Gains Tax at 18 per cent is worked out on the difference between the £31,785 limit of income taxable at the basic rate and Isaac's income of £28,000.

Wherever possible try to utilize your full Capital Gains Tax exemption limit each year. Any unused part of the annual limit is lost. It cannot be carried forward to future years.

By realizing gains just after the end of a tax year you will delay payment of the tax for 12 months.

By splitting sales across the end of a tax year you can make use of your annual exemption limit for two years.

Husband and wife

Husband and wife are:

- separately entitled to the annual exemption limit; and
- individually taxed on chargeable gains they realize in a tax year in excess of the annual exemption limit.

A married couple living together can transfer assets between them without gain or loss as follows:

- The recipient spouse is deemed to have acquired such assets at the cost to the former spouse.
- This exemption ceases when a couple permanently separate.

It is not uncommon for a married couple to own assets in their joint names. For tax purposes, a profit on disposal of a jointly owned asset is apportioned between husband and wife in the ratio of their respective interests in that asset at the date of disposal.

These rules extend to civil partners.

Tax Saver

A husband and wife, or a couple in a Civil Partnership, each have their own annual exemption limit. They should consider transferring assets between them in order to use up both exemption limits.

Tax Saver

But this does not apply to married couples or civil partners who separate. The opportunity to transfer assets between them free of Capital Gains Tax terminates at the end of the tax year in which separation takes place. The moral here is to separate early on in a tax year to allow sufficient time to divide up valuable assets such as land and shares.

Working out chargeable gains

In calculating the taxable gain on the disposal of a chargeable asset, you are allowed to make certain deductions from the proceeds of sale as follows:

- the purchase price;
- incidental costs incurred on acquiring the asset;
- any additional expenditure you have incurred on enhancing the value of the asset, such as improvements or alterations to a property, during your period of ownership; and
- the costs of sale.

The list of incidental expenses that are allowed as either purchase or sale costs includes:

- solicitor's fees, including transfer and conveyancing costs;
- surveyor's, valuer's or auctioneer's fees;

- broker's commission;
- estate agent's commission, including advertising expenses;
- Stamp Duty Land Tax; and
- valuation costs.

Relief for losses

Losses and gains made in the same tax year are offset against each other. Any excess losses can be carried forward, without time limit, to reduce gains in subsequent tax years. But losses can never reduce the amount of your gains to below the annual exemption limit.

Bernard Levy had unused capital losses of £8,100 at 5 April 2015. During 2015/16 he made gains of £23,700 and incurred losses of £10,800. His capital gains position for the year is:

		£	£
Gains realized in the year			23,700
Less: Losses	– in the year	10,800	
	– brought forward (part)	1,800	
			12,600
2015/16 Exemption limit			11,100

The unused losses at 5 April 2016 of £6,300 can be carried forward to be set against gains in later years.

A loss:

- Arising on the sale or gift of an asset to a person with whom you are connected can only be set off against a gain on a similar disposal at a later date.

- Can be claimed where the value of an asset you own becomes negligible or nil. You do not actually have to dispose of the asset. The loss arises on the date that the relief is claimed. In practice, however, a two-year period is allowed from the end of the tax year in which the asset became of negligible value. In some cases the loss can be offset against income, giving you a bigger tax refund.

- On shares you subscribe for in a trading company not quoted on a recognized stock exchange can be set against your income, rather than against other capital gains. This applies whether you realize a loss on disposing of such shares or they become worthless.

Entrepreneurs' Relief

Entrepreneurs' Relief is a relief that can be claimed by individuals in working out their capital gains on the disposal of:

- all or part of a trading business carried on alone or in partnership;
- assets owned by an individual and used in his or her business;
- shares in an individual's own trading company; and
- shares in a trading company where an individual is an employee or officer of the company and:
  - owns at least 5 per cent of the company; or
  - has 5 per cent or more of the voting rights.

The business, assets or shares, as the case may be, must be owned by the individual for at least a year prior to the date of disposal. However, on cessation a three-year time limit is allowed in which to make the disposal providing the individual satisfied the one-year requirement up to cessation.

Under Entrepreneurs' Relief the rate of Capital Gains Tax payable is 10 per cent on your qualifying lifetime gains up to £10 million.

Gains made on disposals before 6 April 2008 do not count towards the lifetime allowance.

Tax Saver

It may pay you to look into how the ownership of your business is structured so that not only you, but also other family members may be entitled to Entrepreneurs' Relief in working out the Capital Gains Tax payable on the profit on a future sale or disposal of the business.

In November 2015 Martin Osborne sold the shares he owned in his own trading company for £460,000. He originally bought the company in 1994 for £190,000. This was his only disposal in 2015/16. Martin pays Capital Gains Tax for the year of £25,890 as follows:

	£
Proceeds of sale	460,000
Less: Purchase price	190,000
Gain qualifying for Entrepreneurs' Relief	270,000
Less: Annual exemption limit	11,100
Gain chargeable to tax	258,900
2015/16 Capital Gains Tax at 10 per cent	£25,890

Assets owned on 31 March 1982

Gains and losses on disposals of assets that you held on 31 March 1982 must be calculated solely by reference to their market value at that date, ignoring original costs.

Ashley Barker acquired a freehold factory in the late 1970s for £25,000. It was valued at £30,000 on 31 March 1982. Ashley sold the factory in May 2015 for £120,000, after expenses of sale.
  The chargeable gain is £90,000 as follows:

	£
Sale price	120,000
Less: March 1982 value	30,000
2014/15 chargeable gain	90,000

Investments in shares

Before 6 April 1982 each shareholding was considered as a single asset and known as a 'pool' of shares. Every purchase of the same class of shares, or a sale of the part of the holding, represented either an addition to, or a disposal out of, the 'pool'. This changed when the indexation allowance was introduced. From 6 April 1982 each shareholding acquired was considered to be a separate asset. A further purchase of shares of a holding owned by you at 5 April 1982 could not be added to the 'pool'.

The rules were amended from 6 April 1985. Shares of the same class were again treated as a single asset growing or diminishing on each acquisition or disposal. This form of 'pooling' applied to shares acquired after 5 April 1982 unless they had already been disposed of before 6 April 1985. It was called a 'new holding'.

A 'pool' that was frozen under the 1982 rules had to stay that way. It continued as a single asset that could not grow by subsequent acquisitions and was known as a '1982 holding'. A '1982 holding' was treated like any other asset in working out entitlement to the indexation allowance. This was not so for a 'new holding'. It had to be continuously indexed each time there was an addition to, or a disposal out of, the 'pool' up until April 1998. All forms of 'pooling' ceased for shares acquired on or after 6 April 1998. This was when indexation was discontinued and replaced by taper relief. From that date until 5 April 2008 it was necessary to record and retain the date of acquisition of each holding of shares.

During this 10-year period the procedure for matching shares sold with their corresponding acquisition was as follows:

- shares acquired on the same day;
- shares acquired within 30 days following a disposal;
- shares acquired before the disposal, but after 5 April 1998, identifying the most recent acquisitions first;
- shares comprised in a 'new holding', the 1982–98 share pool;
- shares within a '1982 holding', the 1965–82 share pool;
- any shares acquired before 6 April 1965, last in first out; or
- shares acquired more than 30 days after the disposal.

Beginning with the 2008/09 tax year:

- following the withdrawal of both indexation and taper relief; and
- having to use the 31 March 1982 value, without exception, in working out capital gains and losses on disposals of assets acquired before that date, a simplified set of identification rules were introduced.

In the following order for shares of the same class that you own, these are:

- shares acquired on the same day;
- shares acquired within 30 days following a disposal; and
- shares in 'a pool', no matter when they were acquired, that grows or diminishes whenever any shares are acquired or disposed of.

Laurence Stone made the following purchases in the shares of a quoted company:

Date	No of shares	Cost
1 June 1978	3,000	£4,500
1 November 1987	3,500	£7,000
1 November 1994	1,500	£5,000
12 August 2015	4,000	£12,000

During 2015/16 he also made the following sales:

Date	No of shares	Sale proceeds
3 September 2015	2,000	£6,600
4 February 2016	6,000	£21,600

The shares were valued at £1.75 on 31 March 1982.

The 2,000 shares sold on 3 September 2015 must, first of all, be identified with part of the acquisition of 4,000 shares on 12 August 2015 as follows:

	£
Proceeds of sale	6,600
Less: cost of 2,000 shares on 12 August 2015	6,000
Chargeable gain	600

The sale of 6,000 shares on 4 February 2016 must be matched with the same number of shares in 'the pool' as follows:

	No of shares	Cost/valuation (£)
Shares acquired on 1 June 1978 (at 31 March 1982 valuation)	3,000	5,250
Purchase in November 1987	3,500	7,000
Additional acquisition 1 September 1994	1,500	5,000
Purchase on 12 August 2015 (remainder)	2,000	6,000
	10,000	23,250
Proceeds of sale of 6,000 shares on 4 February 2016		21,600
Less: deductible cost/value 6,000/10,000 × £23,250		13,950
Chargeable gain		7,650

The 'pool' of the remaining 4,000 shares, with a deductible cost/valuation of £9,300, is carried forward to future years.

The total chargeable gain on Laurence's two sales in 2015/16 is £8,250.

Whenever you receive a free or bonus issue of shares of the same class as an existing holding, the date of their acquisition is the same as that of the original holding. The same principle applies to further shares acquired under a rights issue.

Where a company in which you have a holding is taken over and you receive shares in the new company in exchange for your shares in the company taken over, no disposal for tax purposes takes place at that time. Your new holding is regarded as having being acquired at the same time, and for the same price, as the old one. If, however, you receive a mixture of cash and shares in the new company, a gain or a loss arises on the cash element of the takeover. It is then necessary to apportion the cost price of the old shares between the cash received and the value of the shareholding in the new company at the time.

Your home

The profit on the sale of your home is free of tax. The exemption automatically covers:

- the house; and
- the garden or grounds up to half a hectare, including the land on which the house is built.

A larger area can qualify for exemption where it can be shown that it was required for the enjoyment of the house.

Where a home has not been lived in as your private residence throughout the full period of ownership or, if later, since 31 March 1982, a proportion of the gain on sale is taxable. Certain periods of absence are, however, disregarded in determining whether the gain is totally tax free.

Tax Saver

These are:

- the last 18 months of ownership always; and
- generally when you have to live away from home because of your work.

Guy Robinson sold his home in February 2016, making a profit of £90,000 as worked out for Capital Gains Tax purposes. He had bought the property in November 2009.

His job had taken him abroad between March 2010 and May 2012. Shortly after his return he bought a new home and moved there in August 2012.

The time spent working abroad and the last 18 months from August 2014 are also considered periods when the property was Guy's main residence. The chargeable gain is, therefore, restricted to the part of the gain apportioned to the two years between August 2012 and August 2014 as follows:

$$\frac{\text{Chargeable period}}{\text{Period of ownership}} = \frac{24 \text{ months}}{75 \text{ months}} \times £90,000 = £28,800$$

Where part of your home is used exclusively for business purposes, such as a surgery or office, the proportion of the profit on sale attributable to the business use:

- is a chargeable gain; and
- qualifies for Entrepreneurs' Relief.

Tax Saver

If, during your period of ownership, a property is partly lived in as your home and rented out for the remainder of the time, the gain attributable to the period of letting that is exempt is the lower of:

- either £40,000; or
- an amount equivalent to the gain on the part you have occupied as your home.

Harriet Underwood made a taxable profit of £85,000 when she sold her flat in May 2015. She had acquired the property in April 2008 but only lived there from April 2012 until it was sold. For the remainder of the time the property was rented out. The chargeable gain is £11,000 as follows:

	£	£
Capital gain (period of ownership)		85,000
Less: Main residence exemption – 37 months	37,000	
Letting exemption – 48 months (lower of £40,000 or £37,000)	37,000	
		74,000
Chargeable gain		11,000

A second home

It is not uncommon these days for individuals to have two properties. The main home is usually a house or flat within a commutable distance from the office or other place of work. The second property might be in the country, by the seaside or abroad in a warmer climate.

Tax Saver

It is only the profit on the sale of your main residence that is tax free. Which one of your two or more homes is considered your main residence is usually a matter of fact. It is, however, possible for you to determine this in writing to your tax office. In the election you should state which of your homes you want regarded as your principal private residence for Capital Gains Tax purposes. The election can:

- commence from the date when you first have at least two homes available to you;

- apply from any time in the two years starting with the commencement date;

- be made retrospectively on any date within two years of the commencement date; or

- be varied as and when it suits you.

Husband and wife living together are only allowed one qualifying home between them. The same applies to civil partners.

Tax Saver

However, husband and wife or civil partners should certainly consider owning a second home jointly. This could help reduce the Capital Gains Tax payable on a future sale as they may both be able to take advantage of their respective annual exemption limits in working out the tax payable on a profit on sale.

Pradeep and Sonia Singh bought their first home in January 2010 for £120,000. Not long afterwards Sonia received an inheritance from her father's estate and, with some of the money, they decided to buy a small flat by the seaside. This cost them £70,000 in October 2011. They elected for their first home to be their principal private residence for Capital Gains Tax purposes. In March 2016 they sold their holiday flat for £150,000, realizing a profit of £80,000. In order to reduce their tax bill they changed their main residence election to the holiday flat for the final four weeks up to the date of sale. The taxable gain, split equally between them, is £52,830 as follows:

	£
Profit on sale	80,000
Less: Main residence relief (last 18 months) $\dfrac{18 \text{ months}}{53 \text{ months}} \times £80,000$	27,170
Chargeable gain	52,830

Tax Saver

It is not uncommon for unmarried couples to each own a home. They may each be able to nominate a main residence for the purposes of Capital Gains Tax.

Tax Saver

If you own a home that was occupied rent-free by the same dependent relative both on 5 April 1988 and throughout your period of ownership, then the profit on the sale is tax free.

Chattels

Profits from selling chattels with an expected life of more than 50 years that are sold for less than £6,000 are tax free. Chattels include paintings and other works of art, antiques, furniture, jewellery, stamps and ornaments. Articles comprising a set are considered as a single item when they are sold to the same person but at different times.

For items that fetch between £6,000 and £15,000, the chargeable gain is restricted to 5/3 times the amount by which the proceeds of sale (ignoring expenses) exceeds £6,000 where this is to your advantage.

Meryl Nichols sold an antique vase at auction in March 2016 for £10,500, receiving £9,750 after expenses of sale. She had inherited the vase from her mother when she died in April 1987. It was then valued at only £1,000.

The chargeable gain is £7,500 as follows:

	£
Net sale price	9,750
Less: Acquisition cost	1,000
Profit	8,750
But restricted to 5/3 × £4,500 (£10,500 − £6,000)	7,500

When an article is sold for under £6,000 and at a loss, the allowable loss is restricted by assuming the sale proceeds were equal to £6,000.

Vincent Wells bought a set of stamps in the late 1980s for £8,300. The set was sold in December 2015 for £6,600. Vincent's allowable loss is £1,700. If he had only made £3,800 on the sale, the tax loss would have been £2,300 (£8,300 − £6,000).

Gifts and valuations

There are times when a figure different from the actual disposal proceeds is used in the calculation of a capital gain. This happens, for example, when you make a gift or sell an asset at a nominal value to a close member of your family. On these occasions you must work out the capital gain based on the open-market value of the asset at the time of gift or disposal.

There is a free service from HMRC that will help you whenever you need to use valuations to work out a gain or loss.

After you have made disposal but before you make your return:

- you need to ask for one copy of Form CG34 for each valuation you want checked and confirmed; and
- you must then return the completed form to your tax office at least two months before the filing date for the tax return together with all the other information and documents requested on the form.

Agreed valuations will not subsequently be challenged when you submit your Tax Return unless you did not previously mention important facts affecting the valuations. If your figures are not agreed, HMRC will put forward alternative valuations.

Tax Saver

Where the gift is one of a business asset, you can elect jointly with the transferee for payment of the tax on the gift to be postponed until the asset is subsequently disposed of by the transferee.

Short life assets

Short life, or wasting, assets are those with an expected lifespan of less than 50 years. A gain on the disposal of a wasting asset is worked out in the same way as that on the disposal of any other asset, except that the purchase price wastes away during the expected lifespan of the asset.

Leases of land for less than 50 years are wasting assets. There is a specific formula for calculating the proportion of the purchase price of a lease that can be deducted from the sale proceeds.

The gain or loss on the sale of a wasting asset that is also 'tangible moveable property' is outside of tax.

Part disposals

Where you dispose of only part of an asset that you own:

- You apportion the acquisition cost between the part sold and the fraction retained. This is worked out on a pro-rata basis by reference to the sale proceeds of the part sold and the open-market value of the proportion retained.

- The proportion of cost price of the asset attributable to the part retained can be set against the proceeds on the sale of the remainder at a later date.

- If the part sold is small compared with the value of the whole asset, you can simply deduct the sale proceeds from the acquisition cost. Where the part disposal is one of land, this procedure can be followed so long as the sale proceeds are less than both £20,000 and one-fifth of the value of the remaining land.

Enterprise Investment Scheme

A profit on disposing of qualifying shares under the Enterprise Investment Scheme (EIS) is free of Capital Gains Tax, provided:

- the Income Tax relief originally allowed on the investment has not been withdrawn; and

- the disposal takes place at least three years after the issue of the shares.

If you incur a loss on disposing of qualifying shares you can offset the loss against either:

- capital gains in the same year that the loss is realized; or

- your taxable income in the year of loss, or the previous year.

Tax Saver

It is also possible to defer Capital Gains Tax payable on chargeable gains by reinvesting the gains in qualifying EIS shares. For deferral relief purposes the chargeable gains must be reinvested in the period beginning one year before, and ending three years after, the original disposal. Deferral relief can be claimed:

- along with both Income Tax relief (see Chapter 10) and exemption from Capital Gains Tax (as above) up to an annual investment limit of £1 million;

- on its own as the amount of gains that can be deferred is unlimited; or

- in any other combination you choose within the rules.

If deferral relief is claimed, the original liability to Capital Gains Tax will crystallize when the EIS shares are sold.

Seed Enterprise Investment Scheme

A gain on disposing of shares qualifying under the Seed Enterprise Investment Scheme (SEIS) is not chargeable to Capital Gains Tax provided:

- the Income Tax Relief granted on the investment has not been withdrawn; and
- the disposal does not occur within three years after the shares have been issued.

Tax Saver

You can claim exemption from Capital Gains Tax on half of your capital gains up to a maximum of £100,000 where the profit is re-invested in a SEIS. As a consequence the maximum gains free of Capital Gains Tax are £50,000.

Venture Capital Trusts

A profit on disposal of shares in a Venture Capital Trust (VCT) is exempt from Capital Gains Tax provided:

- the original subscription for the shares disposed of did not exceed the maximum permitted investment limit in the year of purchase, £200,000 for 2015/16; and
- the company qualifies as a VCT both at the time the shares are acquired and at the date of disposal.

Inheritances

No Capital Gains Tax is payable on the unrealized profits on your assets as at the date of your death. When you inherit an asset you acquire it at the value on the date of death of the deceased. Generally, this rule is also applied whenever you become entitled to assets from a Trust.

How to complete your Tax Return and work out your tax

14

This tax guide is being published shortly after HMRC have sent out Tax Returns:

- requiring taxpayers, by law, to make a Return of their taxable income and capital gains for the year from 6 April 2015 to 5 April 2016; and
- enabling them to claim the allowances and tax reliefs to which they are entitled for the same year.

Do I need to complete a Tax Return?

You probably don't need to complete a Tax Return if:

- your tax affairs are not complicated; and
- you receive income taxed under PAYE.

But you may need to fill one in if:

- your tax affairs are not straightforward; and
- you receive income from several sources.

Who has to complete a Tax Return?

HMRC will want a Tax Return from you each year if you:

- are self-employed;

- are a company director;

- own land or property in the United Kingdom from which you receive rents;

- have other untaxed income and it is not possible to collect the tax due through your PAYE tax code;

- make capital gains in excess of the annual exemption limit; or

- are an employee or pensioner with more complex tax affairs.

Employees and pensioners with complex tax affairs

You must fill in a Tax Return if you:

- have an annual income of at least £100,000;

- receive income from savings or investments of at least £10,000 (before tax) in a year;

- have untaxed income in excess of £2,500; or

- owe tax at the end of the year that cannot be collected in the following year through your PAYE tax code.

How do I register for Self Assessment?

HMRC is strongly recommending and encouraging taxpayers to file online because:

- it is secure and convenient;

- tax calculations are done for you automatically;

- on-screen help is available if you need it;

- you get an immediate acknowledgement that your Return has been received; and

- if you are owed money, you will get a faster repayment.

You can also:

- see whether HMRC owe you money, or how much you owe HMRC;
- view your statement of account for the last three years;
- make changes to your personal contact details; and
- make a claim to reduce payments on account or request a refund (if your account is in credit).

You need to visit the GOV.UK website at **www.gov.uk/register-for-self-assessment**:

- if you are not already registered for Self Assessment; and
- to file your tax return online with HMRC's free online service.

You must register by 5 October 2016 if you have to file a tax return for 2015/16. Should you miss this deadline you may become liable to a penalty.

You will need:

- your NINO; and
- information about your business (if applicable).

At the end of the registration process HMRC will give you a Unique Taxpayer Reference (UTR).

To file a tax return online you need an HMRC online account. If you are not given an account when you register you can sign up for one through HMRC's online services.

Filing deadlines

If you decide to complete a paper Tax Return for 2015/16 you must send it back by 31 October 2016 so HMRC has time:

- to work out the tax you owe or the refund due to you; and
- to let you know the result of their calculation before the 31 January 2017 payment deadline.

Tax Saver

Unless your preference is to make a direct payment by 31 January 2017, HMRC will, if possible, collect the tax you owe for the year through next year's tax code so long as they receive your paper 2015/16 Tax Return by 31 October 2016 and you:

- owe tax of not more than £3,000; and
- have a PAYE tax code.

There is no interest or other charge for spreading out the tax under payment for 2015/16 over income received in 2017/18.

The deadline for filing your 2015/16 Return online is 31 January 2017 so if, for example, you miss the 31 October 2016 time limit for paper filing you can still file your Return online by 31 January 2017.

The Tax Return

The Tax Return runs to eight pages. Also available from HMRC are:

- a Tax Return guide;
- supplementary colour-coded pages based on your tax history;
- a separate four-page section of Additional Information pages for dealing with the less common types of income and tax reliefs.

The list of the various supplementary pages is as follows:

Employment	Pink
Self-employment	Orange
Partnership	Turquoise
UK property	Red
Foreign	Mustard
Trusts etc	Brown
Capital gains summary	Blue
Residence, remittance basis etc	Green

Getting started

Try to avoid the temptation of putting off the job of filling in your Return. It is better to get on with it as soon as you can because you will:

- have more time to get help from HMRC if you need it;

- have more time to save for any tax you owe; and

- get a big weight off your mind!

Tax Saver

Getting started as soon as possible is a must if you have paid too much tax. HMRC will refund any overpayment direct to your bank or building society. This is the safest and quickest method. Always fill in boxes 4–14 on page TR6 as appropriate.

Start by going to page TR2. This will help you decide which, if any, supplementary pages you need. These can be obtained by:

- telephoning the order line on 0300 200 3610 (open seven days a week from 8 am to 10 pm); or

- going to **www.gov.uk/self-assessment-forms-and-helpsheets** to download them.

The supplementary pages come with notes to help you fill in the pages you requested. Help sheets that may also further assist you in working out the income or capital gains to be declared on these supplementary pages will be mentioned in the notes and are similarly available from HMRC.

Keeping proper records

Tax Saver

First and foremost, keep proper and orderly records as:

- this will make it easier for you to complete your Tax Return fully and accurately; and

- if the tax office decides to enquire into your Tax Return you will be able to demonstrate that the Return is both accurate and complete from the records you have maintained.

Before you start filling in your Tax Return you need to gather together all the information on your income, capital gains, reliefs and allowances from the records you have been keeping for the year to 5 April 2016. For most types of income and capital gains you only need to retain the records given to you by whoever provided that income or realized the gains for you. This means for those of you:

- In employment:
    - your Form P60, a certificate your employer will give you after 5 April (the end of the tax year) detailing your pay and the tax deducted from it;
    - Form P11D or P9D or equivalent information from your employer showing any benefits-in-kind and expenses payments you received;
    - any Form P45 (part 1A) certificate from an employer showing pay and tax from a job you have left;
    - any Form P160 (part 1A) you may have been given when you retire and then go on to receive a pension from your former employer;
    - your payslips or pay statements;
    - a note of the amount of any tips or gratuities along with details of any other taxable receipts. You are well advised to note these as soon as possible after you receive them, and not simply estimate them at the end of the year.

- Receiving a UK pension or Social Security benefits:
  - your Form P60, a certificate given to you by the payer of your occupational pension, stating the amount of your pension and the tax deducted;
  - a certificate detailing any other pension you received and the tax deducted from it;
  - information given to you by the Department for Work and Pensions (DWP) relating to state pensions, taxable state benefits, statutory sick, maternity or paternity pay and the Jobseeker's Allowance.

- In business or letting property:
  - this is dealt with in the section on records in Chapter 7.

- Receiving investment income:
  - bank and building society statements, passbooks and tax deduction certificates;
  - statements of interest and any other income received from your savings and investments; for example, an annuity;
  - vouchers for dividends received from UK companies;
  - unit trust tax vouchers;
  - life insurance chargeable event certificates;
  - details of any income you received from a trust or the estate of a deceased person;
  - information about any exceptional amounts – such as an inheritance or other windfall – that you receive and subsequently invest.

- Making capital gains or losses:
  - contracts for the purchase or sale of shares, unit trusts, property or any other assets;
  - copies of any valuations you need to work out your capital gains or losses;
  - bills, invoices or other evidence of payment records such as bank statements and cheque stubs for costs you claim for the purchase, improvement or sale of assets;
  - details of any assets you have given away or put into a trust.

- Claiming personal allowances, other deductions or reliefs:
  - certificates of interest paid on any loans that qualify for tax relief;
  - declarations you have made to charities of gifts under Gift Aid;
  - receipts for the payment of pension premiums;
  - notification that you are registered as a blind person.

This list of the types of records you are advised to keep is not exhaustive and does not cover every situation. If you are in any doubt, ask your tax office for assistance.

Tax Saver

Always remember to keep your records for the right length of time. This is:

- the fifth anniversary of 31 January following the tax year if you are self-employed, in partnership or letting property; and

- in any other case the first 31 January anniversary after the tax year.

Filling in your Tax Return

The paper Tax Return is designed to be read by a machine. It is important to complete the form properly so that it is correctly read.

Tax Saver

Always:

- use black ink and capital letters;

- cross out any mistakes and write the correct information below;

- enter figures in whole pounds, ignoring pence;

- round down income;

- round up expenses and tax paid – this will benefit you;

- write in the spaces provided; and

- if a box does not apply simply leave it blank.

There is not enough space for me to reproduce the eight-page Tax Return, as well as the Additional Information and supplementary pages. In the following pages you will find reproductions of the supplementary page on Employment, most of the sections for the Tax Return and some of those from the Additional Information pages.

If you have more than one job you will need to fill in a separate employment page for each job as follows:

- In Box 1 enter your before-tax salary or wage from your P60 or P45.

- Enter the tax taken off your pay in Box 2.

- Tips and other payments not on your P60 go in Box 3.

- The PAYE tax reference of your employer, which will be shown on your P60 or P45, needs to be entered in Box 4.

- Box 5 is for your employer's name.

- Use your Form P11D, or equivalent information, to enter the taxable amounts of any benefits from your employment in Boxes 9 to 16.

- Any business travel or subsistence expenses, professional fees and subscriptions and other expenses paid by you and on which you can claim tax relief go in Boxes 17 to 20.

Leaving aside the sections on the first two pages of the Tax Return asking for your personal details the first part of page TR3 is for you to report your interest and dividend income as follows:

- In Box 1 you should enter the total of the net amount after tax of the interest on all your UK bank, building society and other interest bearing accounts.

- You may have received interest where no tax has been taken off at source. If so, this is the figure to enter in Box 2.

- If you have ever received any interest from overseas not exceeding £2,000, then this amount goes in Box 3.

- It is only the total of all your dividends in the year, excluding tax credits, that should be entered in Box 4.

- You should do likewise in completing Box 5 in respect of any dividends received from authorized unit trusts and open-ended investment companies.

- Boxes 6 and 7 are for your foreign dividends, up to £300, and the tax taken off these foreign dividends.

HM Revenue & Customs

Employment
Tax year 6 April 2015 to 5 April 2016 (2015-16)

Your name	Your Unique Taxpayer Reference (UTR)
SIMON BLACK	4 3 2 9 6 5 5 4 3 4

Complete an 'Employment' page for each employment or directorship

1 Pay from this employment – the total from your P45 or P60 – before tax was taken off
£ 3 4 3 2 0 . 0 0

2 UK tax taken off pay in box 1
£ – 6 7 5 1 . 0 0

3 Tips and other payments not on your P60 – read the 'Employment notes'
£ . 0 0

4 PAYE tax reference of your employer (on your P45/P60)
2 8 / B 6 0 4

5 Your employer's name
BROADWOOD ENGINEERS LTD

6 If you were a company director, put 'X' in the box

6.1 If you ceased being a director before 6 April 2016, put the date the directorship ceased in the box DD MM YYYY

7 And, if the company was a close company, put 'X' in the box

8 If you are a part-time teacher in England or Wales and are on the Repayment of Teachers' Loans Scheme for this employment, put 'X' in the box

Benefits from your employment – use your form P11D (or equivalent information)

9 Company cars and vans – the total 'cash equivalent' amount
£ 3 8 0 0 . 0 0

10 Fuel for company cars and vans – the total 'cash equivalent' amount
£ 4 1 2 3 . 0 0

11 Private medical and dental insurance – the total 'cash equivalent' amount
£ 7 0 0 . 0 0

12 Vouchers, credit cards and excess mileage allowance
£ . 0 0

13 Goods and other assets provided by your employer – the total value or amount
£ . 0 0

14 Accommodation provided by your employer – the total value or amount
£ . 0 0

15 Other benefits (including interest-free and low interest loans) – the total 'cash equivalent' amount
£ . 0 0

16 Expenses payments received and balancing charges
£ . 0 0

Employment expenses

17 Business travel and subsistence expenses
£ . 0 0

18 Fixed deductions for expenses
£ . 0 0

19 Professional fees and subscriptions
£ . 0 0

20 Other expenses and capital allowances
£ . 0 0

ℹ Share schemes, employment lump sums, compensation, deductions and Seafarers' Earnings Deduction are on the 'Additional information' pages.

Interest and dividends from UK banks, building societies etc

1	Taxed UK interest etc - the net amount after tax has been taken off - read the notes
	£ 3 0 4 · 0 0

2	Untaxed UK interest etc - amounts which have not had tax taken off - read the notes
	£ 1 3 0 · 0 0

3	Untaxed foreign interest (up to £2,000) - amounts which have not had tax taken off - read the notes
	£ · 0 0

4	Dividends from UK companies - the net amount, do not include the tax credit - read the notes
	£ 1 2 6 0 · 0 0

5	Other dividends - the net amount, do not include the tax credit - read the notes
	£ 2 8 8 · 0 0

6	Foreign dividends (up to £300) - the amount in sterling after foreign tax was taken off. Do not include this amount in the 'Foreign' pages
	£ 1 6 0 · 0 0

7	Tax taken off foreign dividends - the sterling equivalent
	£ 2 4 · 0 0

The next section on page TR3 deals with UK pensions, annuities and other State benefits received as follows:

- The figure to put in Box 8 is the total of your weekly entitlements to the State Pension, even if you were paid monthly or quarterly. If you do not know the figure, telephone the Pension Direct Service on 0345 606 0265 and ask for a Form BR735 for the year from 6 April 2014 to 5 April 2015. Do not include either the Christmas bonus or your winter fuel payment as these are not taxable.

- You will only need to complete Boxes 9 and 10 if you received a State Pension lump sum in the year.

- All your other pension income, and the tax taken off, needs to be shown in Boxes 11 and 12. In Box 19 on page 7 you should separately list the names of the payers of your pensions, the amounts paid and the tax deducted.

- The remaining boxes are relevant if you are receiving Incapacity Benefit, Contribution-based Employment and Support Allowances, Jobseeker's Allowance or other benefits that are taxable.

UK pensions, annuities and other state benefits received

8 State Pension - amount you were entitled to receive in the year, **not the weekly or 4-weekly amount** - read the notes £ 6 0 2 9 · 0 0	**12** Tax taken off box 11 £ – 2 8 7 3 · 0 0
9 State Pension lump sum - the gross amount of any lump sum - read the notes £ · 0 0	**13** Taxable Incapacity Benefit and contribution-based Employment and Support Allowance - read the notes £ · 0 0
10 Tax taken off box 9 £ · 0 0	**14** Tax taken off Incapacity Benefit in box 13 £ · 0 0
11 Pensions (other than State Pension), retirement annuities and taxable triviality payments – the gross amount. Tax taken off goes in box 12 £ 1 9 0 0 0 · 0 0	**15** Jobseeker's Allowance £ · 0 0
	16 Total of any other taxable State Pensions and benefits £ · 0 0

The final section on page TR3 is for reporting other UK income not included on the supplementary pages and, in most cases, is unlikely to be relevant to your circumstances.

Page TR4 is devoted to tax reliefs, the first part of which is relevant if you want to claim relief for pension contributions. It is likely that the only boxes you will need to complete are Boxes 1 and 2.

Paying into registered pension schemes and overseas pension schemes

Do not include payments you make to your employer's pension scheme which are deducted from your pay before tax or payments made by your employer. If your contributions and other pension inputs are more than the Annual Allowance, you should also fill in boxes 10 to 12 on page Ai 4 of the 'Additional information' pages.

1 Payments to registered pension schemes where basic rate tax relief will be claimed by your pension provider (called 'relief at source'). Enter the payments and basic rate tax £ 2 8 0 0 · 0 0	**3** Payments to your employer's scheme which were not deducted from your pay before tax - this will be unusual - read the notes £ · 0 0
2 Payments to a retirement annuity contract where basic rate tax relief will not be claimed by your provider £ 1 3 6 0 · 0 0	**4** Payments to an overseas pension scheme, which is not UK-registered, which are eligible for tax relief and were not deducted from your pay before tax £ · 0 0

If you pay tax at the higher or additional rates you will be entitled to tax relief on the difference between either 40 per cent or 45 per cent and the basic rate of 20 per cent on your donations to charities under Gift Aid. However, even if you are not claiming this tax relief you should complete the part of the Return on charitable giving as follows:

- The total of all your Gift Aid payments goes in Box 5.
- In Box 6 you need to enter the total of any 'one-off' payments in the figure in Box 5.

- Any Gift Aid donations made in 2015/16 and related back to 2014/15 go in Box 7.

- Perhaps by the time you fill in your Tax Return and send it back to your tax office you have made donations under Gift Aid in the 2016/17 tax year. You can elect to have those payments treated as though they were made in the year to 5 April 2016. Enter the figure in Box 8.

- The value of any shares or securities, land and buildings that you have gifted to charity in the year should be entered in Boxes 9 and 10 respectively.

In Boxes 11 and 12 you should respectively state:

- the value of any investments gifted to non-UK charities in Boxes 9 and 10; and

- Gift Aid payments to non-UK charities in Box 5.

Charitable giving

5 Gift Aid payments made in the year to 5 April 2016 £ **1 8 9 0** · 0 0	9 Value of qualifying shares or securities gifted to charity £ **4 4 7 0** · 0 0
6 Total of any 'one-off' payments in box 5 £ **1 4 1 0** · 0 0	10 Value of qualifying land and buildings gifted to charity £ · 0 0
7 Gift Aid payments made in the year to 5 April 2016 but treated as if made in the year to 5 April 2015 £ **6 6 0** · 0 0	11 Value of qualifying investments gifted to non-UK charities in boxes 9 and 10 £ · 0 0
8 Gift Aid payments made after 5 April 2016 but to be treated as if made in the year to 5 April 2016 £ · **3 1 0** · 0 0	12 Gift Aid payments to non-UK charities in box 5 £ · 0 0

The next tax relief section on page TR4 is only of relevance to you if you can make a claim for the special blind person's allowance. You need to give the name of the local authority, or equivalent body, with whom you have registered your blindness.

Blind Person's Allowance

13 If you are registered blind, or severely sight impaired, and your name is on a local authority or other register, put 'X' in the box **X**	**15** If you want your spouse's, or civil partner's, surplus allowance, put 'X' in the box
14 Enter the name of the local authority or other register **TOPMARSH COUNCIL**	**16** If you want your spouse, or civil partner, to have your surplus allowance, put 'X' in the box

ℹ️ Other less common reliefs are on the 'Additional information' pages.

Page TR5 is concerned with:

- student loan repayments;
- High Income Child Benefit Charge; and
- the new marriage allowance.

You will only need to complete the High Income Child Benefit Charge section if:

- your income was over £50,000 in 2015/16;
- you or your spouse/partner received Child Benefit in the year to 5 April 2016; and
- for couples only – your income was more than that of your spouse/partner.

High Income Child Benefit Charge

Fill in this section if all of the following apply:

- your income was over £50,000
- you or your partner (if you have one) got Child Benefit (this also applies if someone else claims Child Benefit for a child who lives with you and pays you or your partner for the child's upkeep)
- **couples only** - your income was higher than your partner's.

Please read the notes. Use the calculator at **www.gov.uk/child-benefit-tax-calculator** to help you work out the Child Benefit payments you received.

If you have to pay this charge for the 2016-17 tax year and you do not want us to use your 2016-17 PAYE tax code to collect that tax during the year, put 'X' in box 3 on page TR 6.

1 Enter the total amount of Child Benefit you and your partner got for the year to 5 April 2016 £ **1 7 8 8** · 0 0	**3** Enter the date that you and your partner stopped getting all Child Benefit payments if this was before 6 April 2016 DD MM YYYY
2 Enter the number of children you and your partner got Child Benefit for on 5 April 2016 **2**	

Perhaps your income in 2015/16 was under £10,600? If so, you can cut the tax bill of your spouse/partner by transferring £1,060 of your personal allowance to them. But to do so all of the following must apply:

- You were both born after 5 April 1935.

- You were married to, or in a civil partnership with, the same person for all or part of 2015/16.

- The income of your spouse or civil partner in 2015/16 was no more than £42,385.

Marriage Allowance

Please read the notes. If your income for the year ended 5 April 2016 was less than £10,600 you can transfer £1,060 of your Personal Allowance to your spouse or civil partner to reduce the amount of tax they pay if all of the following apply:
- you were married to, or in a civil partnership with, the same person for all or part of the tax year
- you were **both born on or after 6 April 1935**
- your spouse or civil partner's income was less than £42,386

Fill in this section if you want to make the transfer:

1 Your spouse or civil partner's first name	4 Your spouse or civil partner's date of birth DD MM YYYY
SIMON	06 08 1952

2 Your spouse or civil partner's last name	5 Date of marriage or civil partnership DD MM YYYY
BLACK	19 05 1978

3 Your spouse or civil partner's National Insurance number
BZ 62 24 17 A

Pages TR6 onwards are all about finishing off your Tax Return. However, before you do so, you may need to complete some of the sections on the Additional Information pages, which are for less common types of income, deductions and tax reliefs, and for other information. The second section on page Ai2 is for you to claim other tax reliefs, such as:

- Your subscriptions for new ordinary shares in a Venture Capital Trust go in Box 1.

- Box 2 is for your subscriptions for shares issued under the Enterprise Investment Scheme.

- The total of your qualifying loan interest payable in the year should be entered in Box 5.

- Maintenance or alimony payments you are making, subject to a maximum of £3,220, should be entered in Box 7, but only if you or your former spouse or civil partner was born before 6 April 1935.

- In Box 10 you should put the amount of your subscriptions for shares under the Seed Enterprise Investment Scheme.

Then follows a section on the married couple's allowance. You should carefully read the notes at the top of page Ai3 before completing Boxes 1 to 11 as appropriate.

The second part of this page is devoted to Income Tax losses and the limit of Income Tax relief on these losses (see Chapter 7).

Other tax reliefs – read the notes

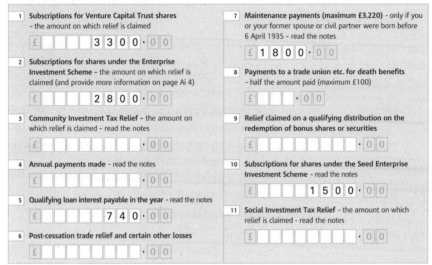

1 Subscriptions for Venture Capital Trust shares – the amount on which relief is claimed

£ 3 3 0 0 · 0 0

2 Subscriptions for shares under the Enterprise Investment Scheme – the amount on which relief is claimed (and provide more information on page Ai 4)

£ 2 8 0 0 · 0 0

3 Community Investment Tax Relief – the amount on which relief is claimed – read the notes

£ · 0 0

4 Annual payments made – read the notes

£ · 0 0

5 Qualifying loan interest payable in the year - read the notes

£ 7 4 0 · 0 0

6 Post-cessation trade relief and certain other losses

£ · 0 0

7 Maintenance payments (maximum £3,220) - only if you or your former spouse or civil partner were born before 6 April 1935 - read the notes

£ 1 8 0 0 · 0 0

8 Payments to a trade union etc. for death benefits – half the amount paid (maximum £100)

£ · 0 0

9 Relief claimed on a qualifying distribution on the redemption of bonus shares or securities

£ · 0 0

10 Subscriptions for shares under the Seed Enterprise Investment Scheme - read the notes

£ 1 5 0 0 · 0 0

11 Social Investment Tax Relief - the amount on which relief is claimed - read the notes

£ · 0 0

You are probably now in a position to put the finishing touches to your Tax Return. If you want to calculate your tax you will have to ask HMRC for the Tax Calculation Summary pages and notes that will help you work out:

- any tax due or repayable; and
- if payments on account are necessary.

There is a choice of boxes to complete if you have not paid enough tax:

- Box 2 covers tax due for 2015/16 and the alternative methods of payment if you owe less than £3,000.
- Box 3 deals with the collection of tax for 2016/17 on your savings income and/or the High Income Child Benefit Charge.

But if you have overpaid you need to give the information requested in Boxes 4 to 14 on page TR6 of the bank or building society account into which you would like the tax refund paid.

Do not miss the deadline for filing your Tax Return because, perhaps, you are waiting for some final figures. Use estimates and make sure you send the correct figures as soon as you can. You should tick Box 20 on page TR8 of your Return and describe in the space provided at Box 19:

- which figures are provisional (you should refer to the appropriate box numbers on your Tax Return or any other supplementary pages you have completed);
- why you could not give final figures; and
- when you expect to be able to provide your tax office with the correct information.

Put 'X' in Box 21 if you are enclosing separate supplementary pages. You must then sign and date the Return in Box 22. Have regard to the wording of the declaration:

'I declare the information I have given on this Return and any supplementary pages is correct and complete to the best of my knowledge and belief. I understand that I may have to pay financial penalties and face prosecution if I give false information.'

The form and any supplementary pages are now ready to send back to your tax office.

Working out your tax

The key steps in calculating your tax bill are as follows:

1 Add up all the non-savings income you have entered on your Return.

2 Total the allowances and other deductions you have claimed for the year but excluding those such as personal pension premiums and donations under Gift Aid paid net of tax at the basic rate.

3 Take (2) away from (1).

4 Work out the tax due on (3) but increasing the basic rate band of £31,785 by the grossed up equivalent of personal pension and Gift Aid payments.

5 If you are taxable at the higher or additional rates of 40 per cent and 45 per cent, work out the additional tax payable on your savings income and dividends.

6 Add (4) and (5) together.

7 If you are self-employed or in partnership, work out how much you owe for Class 4 National Insurance Contributions.

8 Add (6) and (7) together and take away all tax deducted at source.

This is your tax bill unless you also owe tax on capital gains realized in excess of your annual exemption limit. You will then be able to:

- work out what tax you have to pay for 2015/16 due on 31 January 2017; and

- calculate any payments on account for 2016/17 payable on 31 January and 31 July 2017.

Illustration

Celia Mercer, who is single, is employed as a fashion designer. She frequently has to travel so her employer provides her with a company car, fuel for private mileage as well as private medical insurance cover.

In her spare time Celia speaks at trade shows. She also writes articles for fashion magazines.

A few years ago Celia's mother died. The inheritance she received is invested in a portfolio of shares. She also owns a buy-to-let flat and has spare cash deposited in building society accounts.

Celia filed her Tax Return for the year to 5 April 2016 online on 22 November 2016. It shows the following entries:

	£	Page no	Box no
(1) Employment			
Salary	50,000	E1	1
Tax deducted by employer	12,417	E1	2
Company car benefit	3,200	E1	9
Car fuel benefit	3,536	E1	10
Medical insurance	800	E1	11
(2) Self-employment			
Adjusted profit shown by the accounts for the year to 30 September 2015	7,000	SEF4	75
(3) UK property			
Net rental income from buy-to-let flat	4,500	UKP2	38
(4) UK interest and dividends			
Building Society interest	1,200	TR3	1
Dividends from UK companies	1,620	TR3	4
(5) Reliefs			
Personal pension premiums	2,200	TR4	1
Interest on loan to buy investment flat	3,100	Ai2	5
(6) Capital gains			
In excess of annual exemption limit	1,600	CG1	8

The calculation of Celia's tax liability for 2015/16 is as follows:

Income received (before tax taken off)	£	£	£
Pay, business profits and letting income	69,036		
Interest received from UK banks and building societies	1,500		
Dividends from UK companies (plus 10% tax credits)	1,800		
Total income received		72,336	
Less: Personal allowance	10,600		
Interest on buy-to-let loan	3,100		
Total		13,700	
Total income on which tax is due		58,636	
Tax thereon:			
Pay, business profit and letting income		34,535 @ 20 per cent =	6,907.00
		20,801 @ 40 per cent =	8,320.40
Bank and building society interest		1,500 @ 40 per cent =	600.00
Dividend income		1,800 @ 32.5 per cent =	585.00
Income Tax charged			16,412.40
Less: 10% tax credits on dividends from UK companies (not repayable)			182.00
			16,230.40
Less: Tax deducted			
Interest received from UK banks and building societies		300.00	
Salary		12,417.00	
			12,717.00
			3,513.40
Add: Capital Gains Tax: £1,600 @ 28 per cent			448.00
Tax due for 2015/16			3,961.40

Tax payments

Tax due for 2015/16 (as above)	3,961.40
Payment on account made 31 January 2016	(1,500.00)
Payment on account made 31 July 2016	(1,500.00)
Balance due for 2015/16	961.40
Add: First payment on account for 2016/17	1,756.70
Amount due on 31 January 2017	£2,718.10
Second payment on account for 2016/17	1,756.70
Amount due on 31 July 2017	£1,756.70

Notes

1 Celia's employment income comprises her salary of £50,000 and taxable benefits of £7,536.

2 The band of income taxable at the basic rate is extended by the grossed up equivalent of the personal pension premiums of £2,200 from £31,785 by £2,750 to £34,535.

3 Celia applied for, and was granted, permission to defer payment of Class 4 National Insurance Contributions.

4 Tax payments of £1,500 were made by Celia on both 31 January and 31 July 2016 based on her tax liability for 2014/15.

5 In working out her payments on account for 2016/17 Celia does not need to include her Capital Gains Tax liability for 2015/16 of £448.

What HMRC do

When your complet ed Tax Return is received by your tax office it will be processed as quickly as possible based on your entries on the Return. Any simple straightforward mistakes will be corrected by HMRC and you will be told about them.

You will then be sent a calculation of your tax position if you have asked HMRC to work this out for you. Alternatively, if you have calculated your own tax bill and it is incorrect, HMRC will send you their tax calculation.

Some other hints on efficient tax compliance

Tax Saver

Always remember that both send-back dates of 31 October (for paper) and 31 January (online) are critical. You must stick to them otherwise you will come within the penalty regime for the late filing of the Return.

Tax Saver

If the amount of any of your sources of income is substantially different compared to the previous year, use the Additional Information box on page TR6 to explain the reason for the change.

Tax Saver

Do not forget to sign the Return. This is one of the most common mistakes that HMRC have found when processing Tax Returns.

Tax Saver

Remember that you can amend your Self Assessment at any time in the 12-month period after the latest 31 January deadline.

Tax Saver

Remember the key dates in the Self Assessment calendar, which are summarized in Appendix 7 on page 268.

Paying your tax, interest and penalties

15

Under the Self Assessment tax system:

- there are specified dates each year when you must pay your tax; and
- you regularly receive a Statement of Account from HMRC detailing both tax recently paid and the next amount due.

Tax payment dates

The tax payment dates for 2015/16 are:

		Due date for tax payments on account	Due date for final balance
Rental income and untaxed investment income			
Business profits	50%	31/01/2016	31/01/2017
Unpaid PAYE (where not coded)	50%	31/07/2016	
Higher and additional rate tax on investment income (taxed at source)			
Capital Gains Tax		N/A	31/01/2017

The one exception to the rule requiring direct payment of tax to HMRC relates to employees or pensioners who owe less than £3,000 in tax. They can choose to have the amount collected monthly in the following year through the PAYE system:

- by filing a paper return at their tax office no later than 31 October following the end of the tax year; or
- by filing online by 30 December after the end of the tax year.

Payments on account

As the table above shows, some taxpayers, mainly those who are self-employed, will make two payments on account of the tax due for a year on:

- 31 January in the tax year; and
- 31 July following the end of the tax year.

Payments on account are worked out by splitting into two equal amounts the tax paid for the previous tax year (after taking off tax incurred at source and any Capital Gains Tax).

You do not need to make payments on account of Income Tax if:

- the amount you owe for Income Tax and Class 4 National Insurance Contributions for the previous tax year – after taking off tax paid at source on, for example, dividends, bank and building society interest – is less than £1,000; or
- at least 80 per cent of your Income Tax and Class 4 National Insurance Contributions bill for the preceding tax year was represented by tax deducted from the income before you received it.

It follows that most employees and pensioners will not have to make the half-yearly payments on account.

Reduced payments on account

Maybe, because of a change in your financial circumstances (particularly in view of the present difficult economic climate), your payments on account for the tax year (based on what you paid in the previous year) point towards an overstatement of your likely liability for the year.

This might happen where you expect:

- your income in 2016/17 to be lower than that in 2015/16;
- your allowances or reliefs to be higher; and
- that more of your income will incur tax at source in 2016/17, because:
  - it will be taxed under PAYE; or
  - your savings income taxed at source will increase.

Tax Saver

In such circumstances you can claim to reduce your payments on account. You do this by using Form SA303, which is available online or from your tax office. The form gives guidance on how to complete it.

If the claim to reduce your payments on account subsequently turns out to be excessive then you will be asked to pay interest on the difference between the reduced tax you actually paid and the payments on account that should have been made.

Statements of Account

At the top of your Self Assessment Statement you will see:

- the Statement number and date of issue;
- your 10-digit Unique Taxpayer Reference number (UTR);
- your National Insurance Number (NINO); and
- your employer's tax reference, if you are employed.

The Statement then goes on to document:

- the opening balance, if any, brought forward from the previous Statement;
- what has happened since the last Statement; and
- whether there is an over-payment or, most probably, an amount to pay, and when to pay it. This is shown in a summary box at the end of the Statement.

If you are making payments on account you can expect to receive the following Statements up to February 2017:

July 2016	To tell you of the second payment on account 2015/16 due on 31 July 2016.
August 2016	To let you know of any outstanding balance of the second payment on account. The statement will also include a figure for interest due to date.
January 2017	To advise you of your balancing payment for 2015/16 and your first payment on account for 2016/17, both due on 31 January 2017.
February 2017	To show any outstanding amounts that should have been paid on 31 January 2017. The statement will also include a charge for interest due to date.

You will also receive a Statement of Account:

- whenever there is a change to the amount of tax you owe; and
- where you are due a refund from HMRC.

Other points of interest are:

- As HMRC carry out security checks, any tax refund due to you may not actually be issued until some time after the date shown on your Statement of Account.
- Where a tax liability will shortly be due for payment, HMRC will usually set any tax refund against this amount and then just repay the balance.
- If you have made a payment in the short period before you receive a Statement, it will appear on the next one.

If you have registered for Self Assessment online you can access a wide range of services, including:

- viewing the latest issued copy of your Statement, as well as any Statements issued to you in the last three years;
- viewing payments/credits and how these have been allocated;

- viewing liabilities by tax year, including interest, penalties and surcharges;
- requesting repayments where an account is in credit;
- claiming to reduce payments on account;
- viewing and changing your address; and
- paying by direct debit online.

Paying your tax

There are a number of secure and efficient methods for paying your tax recommended by HMRC. If you use payment by post you should:

- make your cheque out to 'HM Revenue & Customs Only' followed by your Unique Taxpayer Reference; and
- send it to HMRC in the return envelope accompanied by the tear-off payment slip from your Statement of Account.

A stamp for the correct postage is needed. If you do not have a return envelope, your cheque should be sent to HMRC Bradford, BD98 1YY.

HMRC politely request that:

- your cheque and the tear-off payment slip be unfolded;
- you do not staple or attach paperclips to cheques; and
- you do not pay your tax by sending cash through the post.

You can assist your accounts office in dealing promptly with your tax payment by:

- including a separate letter if you are sending a post-dated cheque, or want to give further information about your payment; and
- paying on time – you will not then incur interest charges.

You can also pay:

- using the internet or telephone;
- at a post office or your bank;
- by debit card (Switch, Solo, Electron or Visa Delta) over the internet; or
- by direct debit. This service is available online. You have a choice of setting up either a Single Payment or a Budget Payment Plan.

Many of us:

- already use direct debit to make regular payments for household and other costs; and

- are familiar with the advantages of paying by direct debit.

Under the Budget Payment Plan, which is voluntary, you can make regular payments towards a future tax liability. The plan is flexible and you:

- decide the regular weekly or monthly amount you want to pay to HMRC;

- can choose to amend your regular payment amount;

- are free to take a break or suspend payment for a period of up to six months; and

- can cancel the Budget Payment Plan at any time.

The payments you make:

- are in advance; and

- reduce what you have to pay on either the following 31 January or 31 July.

You must still pay the full amount of tax by the due date.

Certificates of tax deposit

You can provide for the payment of a future tax liability by purchasing a Certificate of Tax Deposit. The main features of such certificates are:

- the minimum first deposit is £500;

- subsequent deposits must be at least £250;

- they earn interest from the date of purchase to the normal due date for payment of the tax; and

- the interest is taxable.

Business Payment Support Service

Tax Saver

In response to economic conditions HMRC has introduced a Business Support Service dedicated to assist businesses with temporary cash flow problems.

If you are concerned:

- about being able to meet tax, National Insurance or other payments due to HMRC; or

- that future payments could cause you difficulties,

you can get in touch with HMRC to discuss payment options.

You will be asked for the following information:

- your tax reference number;

- details of the tax that you are having or will have trouble paying; and

- an outline summary of the income and expenses of your business.

This will enable HMRC staff to review your particular circumstances and discuss temporary options relevant to the needs of your business, which could for example include allowing you to make tax payments over a longer period. You will not be charged late payment surcharges in such an arrangement although interest will continue to accrue on payments made beyond their due and payable date.

The number to telephone if you need assistance is 0300 200 3835.

What if I can't pay my tax?

If you are unable to settle your tax bill you should speak to the office which sent you the most recent communication. They should be able to help you by:

- giving you extra time to pay; or
- allowing you to settle it in instalments.

HMRC has several options when you fail to:

- reach an agreement; or
- maintain the payments you said you would make.

These are:

- seizing most of your possessions for sale at auction.
- Magistrates or County Court proceedings.
- making you bankrupt.

Date of receipt

Tax payments are considered to be received by the accounts office as follows:

Payment method	Effective date of payment
Received by post (except below)	Day of receipt by HMRC
Received by post following a day when the office has been closed for whatever reason (including a weekend)	The day the office was first closed (for payments received on Monday, the effective date will be the previous Saturday)
Electronic Funds Transfer (EFT) – payment by BACS or CHAPS (Clearing House Automated Payment System)	One working day immediately before the date that the value is received (a working day is defined as a Bank of England working day)
Bank Giro or Girobank	The date on which payment was made at the bank or post office

Interest

You will be charged late payment interest if you do not pay your tax when it is due; and on any penalties based on the overdue tax.

The interest is calculated from the date on which the tax becomes due and payable until payment is made.

The interest rate is Bank Base Rate plus 2.5 per cent. At the time of going to print this works out at 3 per cent. Tax relief on the interest is not allowed.

There may be circumstances when the imposition of interest would not be fair to you and can be justifiably contested. HMRC's Code of Practice (No 1) sets out the circumstances in which HMRC will consider setting aside a change to interest in overdue tax where there has been an undue delay on their part.

You will be paid interest, which is called repayment interest and is not taxable, by HMRC on overpayment of any of the following:

- payments on account of Income Tax;
- Income tax and Capital Gains Tax; and
- any penalties imposed.

The formula for working out the interest rate on repayments is Bank Base Rate minus 1 per cent but with a minimum rate of 0.5 per cent.

Remission of tax

Arrears of Income Tax or Capital Gains Tax may be waived if they result from HMRC's failure to make proper and timely use of information supplied by:

- the taxpayer about his or her own income, capital gains or personal circumstances;
- an employer, where the information affects an employee's notice of coding; or
- the DWP about a taxpayer's retirement, disability or widow's State Pension.

The concession is normally only given where the taxpayer:

- could reasonably have believed that his or her tax affairs were in order; and
- is notified of the arrears by the end of the tax year following that in which it arose.

Late payment penalty

A late payment penalty is levied on the late payment of Income Tax, but not payments on account, or Capital Gains Tax as follows:

Tax unpaid by 3 March* (30 days after the tax was due)	5% of unpaid tax
Tax unpaid by 3 August* (5 months after the initial penalty was imposed)	Further 5% of tax unpaid
Tax unpaid by 3 February* (11 months after the initial penalty was imposed)	Further 5% of tax unpaid

* these dates will be one day earlier when the 31 January falls in a leap year.

A penalty notice must be formally served on you by HMRC. You have 30 days in which to appeal against the notice if you think you have a reasonable excuse for the late payment of the tax. Your appeal might be successful:

- if there is clear evidence that your cheque was lost in the post; or
- in the event of serious illness.

Examples of circumstances where your appeal will be rejected are:

- cheques wrongly made out; and
- lack of funds other than for exceptional reasons.

Penalties

The main penalties under Self Assessment are:

Offence	Penalty
You do not submit a paper Tax Return to your tax office by 31 October after the end of the tax year	£100
Your do not file online by 31 January after the end of the tax year	£100
Your Return is more than three months late	An automatic penalty of £10 a day up to a maximum of £900
Your Return is more than six months late	A tax geared penalty that is the greater of 5% of the tax due and £300
Your Return is still outstanding after a year	Another tax geared penalty that again is the greater of 5% of the tax due and £300
	In particularly serious cases a higher penalty of up to 100% of the tax due can be imposed.

It is important to note that the time limits for the imposition of these late filing penalties run from:

- 31 October for paper returns; and
- 31 January for online filers.

Where taxpayers have a genuinely good excuse for missing the annual filing deadline for submitting Tax Returns they can appeal against the automatic late filing penalty.

What may be accepted by HMRC as a reasonable excuse for late filing include:

- where the Tax Return was not received by the taxpayer;
- where the Tax Return was lost in the post or delayed because of:
  - a fire or flood at the post office where the Tax Return was handled;
  - prolonged industrial action within the post office; or
  - an unforeseen event that disrupted the postal services.
- where a taxpayer lost his or her tax records as a result of fire, flood or theft;
- serious illness; and
- death of a spouse, domestic partner or close relative.

HMRC will not agree the following as a reasonable excuse for being late:

- Tax Return too difficult;
- pressure of work;
- lack of information; or
- absence of reminders from HMRC.

The other penalties are:

Offence	Penalty
You do not receive a Tax Return and fail to notify HMRC of chargeability to tax within six months of the end of the tax year	% of the tax payable: (a) None if the failure is not deliberate (b) 30% for a careless oversight (c) 70% for a deliberate but not concealed failure (d) 100% if the failure was both deliberate and concealed
Failure to maintain and keep records	Up to £3,000
Fraudulently or negligently claiming to reduce interim tax payments	Up to an amount equivalent to the difference between the tax paid and the tax that should have been paid

Generally a penalty determination must be made, or proceedings commenced, within six years of the date on which the penalty was incurred. The rules allow for this period of time to be extended to any later date within three years of the final determination of the tax liability.

The penalty regime for errors on documents and returns depends on:

- why you made the error; and

- how serious the reason was.

HMRC use penalties to stop individuals who do not take care with their tax affairs from gaining an unfair advantage. If you take reasonable care to get it right, HMRC will not charge a penalty where an error occurs. Some of the ways you can demonstrate you took reasonable care are:

- keeping accurate records and updating them regularly so you can make sure your Tax Returns are correct;

- saving your records should you need them at a later date;

- checking what the correct position is when you do not understand something or, alternatively, seeking advice from HMRC or a competent tax adviser; and

- telling HMRC as soon as possible about any error you discover after sending in a tax return or other document.

If you do not take reasonable care HMRC can penalize any errors and penalties will be higher if the errors are deliberate.

What if you have to pay a penalty? HMRC will:

- Contact you to discuss your tax.

- Discuss the reason for the error – the more serious the reason, the higher the tax penalty can be.

- Reduce the penalty if you help them work out the correct tax due.

- Explain why they are issuing a penalty and will send you a penalty notice. HMRC can substantially reduce any penalty due if you:

  - tell HMRC about any errors without being prompted by them;

  - help HMRC work out if any extra tax is due; and

  - allow them to check your figures.

The penalty is a percentage of the extra tax due and depends on why you made the error, as follows:

Reason	Rate of penalty	
	Maximum	Minimum
Reasonable care	No penalty	
Carelessness	30%	0%
Deliberate	70%	20%
Deliberate and concealed	100%	30%

You will have to pay the tax and any interest due, as well as the penalty.

If you incur a penalty because you failed to take reasonable care with your tax affairs, HMRC can suspend it for up to two years. In that time you need to get your systems right. If you then meet all the conditions laid down by HMRC the penalty will be cancelled.

You always have the right of appeal where you think that a penalty is unfair.

Elections and claims: time limits

16

You will already have gathered that certain options available to you as a taxpayer are dependent on your submitting an election or making a claim to HMRC. As these will usually involve a saving in tax it is important to appreciate that you often need to act within prescribed time limits. This chapter brings together those elections and claims that are most likely to be of relevance to you. It also sets out the time limit for submission to HMRC. It is by no means exhaustive.

Chapter 2 – Tax rates, allowances and reliefs

Election/claim	Time limit
The various elections for the transfer of the married couple's and blind person's allowances	Generally before the start of the tax year for which it is to have effect
Claim to the personal allowances detailed in the chapter	No later than four years after 31 January next following the end of the tax year
Transfer of excess allowances between husband and wife	No later than four years after 31 January next following the end of the tax year

Chapter 3 – Tax credits

Election/claim	Time limit
Claims for tax credits	Claims will only be backdated by a maximum of one month
Annual renewal	By 31 July following the end of a tax year

Chapter 4 – Interest payments and other outgoings

Election/claim	Time limit
Election to treat charity donations under Gift Aid as made in the previous tax year	On or before when you deliver your tax return for the previous year after the tax year

Chapter 6 – Value Added Tax

Election/claim	Time limit
Application for registration	No later than 30 days from the end of the month after the one when turnover exceeds the registration limit
Claim for bad debt relief	When a debt remains unpaid for more than six months

Chapter 7 – Working for yourself

Election/claim	Time limit
Cash accounting for a small business	Tick box on page SEF1 of the Tax Return
Relief for post-cessation expenses	No later than one year after 31 January next following the tax year in which the payments are made
Creating a separate pool to work out the capital allowances on an asset with a short life expectancy	No later than one year after 31 January next following the tax year in which the period of account ended in which the expenditure is incurred
Relief for the loss sustained in the tax year against other income of the same year or the preceding year	Within one year after 31 January next following the tax year in which the loss arose
Relief for a trading loss against the profits arising from the same trade in subsequent periods	Within four years after 31 January next following the tax year in which the loss was sustained
Relief for the loss in the first four years of assessment of a new business to be given against the income of the three preceding years of assessment	No later than one year after 31 January next following the tax year in which the loss occurred
Relief for trading losses to be offset against capital gains	No later than one year after 31 January next following the tax year
Relief for the loss in the last 12 months of trading to be given against the profits of the same trade that were assessed in the three tax years prior to the year in which the trade was discontinued.	Within four years after 31 January next following the tax year in which the trade ceased

Chapter 10 – Savings and investment income

Election/claim	Time limit
An election to opt out of rent-a-room relief for a particular tax year, or withdrawal of an election	Within one year after 31 January next following the tax year
An election for the alternative basis of rent-a-room relief, or revocation of an election	Within one year after 31 January next following the tax year
Claim for Income Tax relief under the Enterprise Investment Scheme	Within four years after 31 January next following that in which the shares were issued
Claim for Income Tax relief under the Seed Enterprise Investment Scheme	Within four years after 31 January next following that in which the shares were issued
Declaration by a married couple or civil partners that their beneficial interest in joint property and the income arising from it are unequal	The date of the declaration, which must be sent to HMRC within 60 days

Chapter 13 – Capital gains

Election/claim	Time limit
Claim to the capital loss where the value of an asset becomes negligible	The loss arises on the date of claim although, in practice, a two-year period is allowed from the end of the tax year in which the asset became of negligible value
Claim for the loss on shares that were originally subscribed for in an unquoted trading company to be set against income in the year of loss, or the preceding year	No later than one year after 31 January next following the tax year in which the loss was made
Claim to Entrepreneurs' Relief	No later than one year after 31 January next following the tax year in which the disposal took place
An election to determine which of your homes is to be regarded as your principal residence for Capital Gains Tax purposes	Two years from the date when two or more properties are eligible

Inheritance Tax

17

Inheritance Tax is payable on:

- any chargeable transfers you make during your lifetime; and
- the value of your estate on death.

There are a number of exemptions and reliefs that, if optimized, can reduce the amount of tax payable, perhaps significantly.

As with all types of direct taxation, husband, wife and civil partners are all treated as separate individuals.

Inheritance Tax is administered by the inheritance tax offices of HMRC in England and Scotland, to whom all Returns, Accounts and payments of tax should be submitted.

Some of the aspects of the tax, particularly those relating to agricultural and business property as well as transfers into Trusts, are complex. Therefore, what follows is a summary of the main areas of the tax that are likely to be of most relevance and interest to you.

Potentially exempt transfers

Perhaps the most significant feature of Inheritance Tax is that of a potentially exempt transfer (PET). This is:

- an outright gift to an individual;
- a gift into settlement for the benefit of a disabled person; or
- certain other transfers into Trust.

No tax is payable providing the donor survives for at least seven years from the date of making the gift.

Chargeable lifetime gifts

Any gift or transfer that is not potentially exempt is liable to Inheritance Tax when it is made. Typically, many gifts into settlement are chargeable transfers. In working out the Inheritance Tax at the date of gift:

- it is only the excess, if any, over the nil rate band on which tax is payable; and
- the rate of tax is one-half of the rate applicable on death at the time.

Gifts with reservation and pre-owned assets

If you make a gift but carry on enjoying some benefit from the property or asset, it is still likely to be regarded as yours until either:

- the date when you stop enjoying any benefit from the gift; or
- your death.

This is what is known as a 'gift with reservation'.

You also have to pay income tax each year on the value of any assets that you continue to use or enjoy after you have given them away.

Exemptions

The main exemptions for individuals are:

- Transfers, without limit, between husband and wife – both during lifetime and on death.
- Similarly between civil partners.
- Gifts up to £3,000 in any one tax year. Any part of the exemption that is unused can be carried forward, but to the following year only.

Nancy Young gave her brother £1,800 in August 2014. A year later, she wanted to make a more substantial gift, but this time to her sister. She was able to give away £4,200 in September 2015, within her annual exemption limits for 2014/15 and 2015/16 as follows:

	£
2014/15	
Annual exemption limit	3,000
Less: Gift to brother	1,800
Carried forward to next year	1,200
2015/16	
Annual exemption limit	3,000
Add: Exemption unused in 2014/15	1,200
Available exemption for the year	4,200
Gift to sister	4,200

If Nancy had given her brother £3,000 in August 2014, she would have been limited to gifting the same amount to her sister in 2015/16.

Tax Saver

Using your annual exemption can save £1,200 of Inheritance Tax each year – £2,400 for a couple. Over a period of 10 years, for example, this amounts to a £12,000 reduction in the tax payable on your death, increasing to £24,000 for a couple.

- Gifts to any number of persons, but only up to £250 per person in each tax year. Where the total amount given to any one individual exceeds the amount of £250 then no part of the gift comes within the exemption.
- Marriage gifts. The amount you can give away in consideration of marriage or civil partnership depends on your relationship to the bride, groom or civil partner, as follows:

	£
By either parent	5,000
By a grandparent or great grandparent	2,500
By any other person	1,000

- Regular gifts out of income that form part of your normal expenditure.

> Glyn Fielding, who lives alone, has an annual after-tax income of around £30,000. He has a modest lifestyle. He spends about £20,000 a year on his home, food, recreation, holidays and other living expenses.
>
> His brother, Luke, who is married, is not so fortunate. Glyn could make regular gifts to his brother out of his annual surplus income of £10,000, free of Inheritance Tax.
>
> Over 10 years Glyn might save £40,000 in Inheritance Tax.

- Lifetime gifts and bequests on death to charities and 'qualifying' political parties, without limit.

Your home

These days many of us feel an increasing need to help our children:

- meet the costs of university or other further education; and
- later on in life, towards a deposit on a home.

Perhaps you can only look to your home, where the greatest part of your wealth is tied up, as a source of funds to help your children? But how and what you do with your home has ramifications for Inheritance Tax. If:

- you gift your home and move out you can come back to visit or make short stays without incurring an Inheritance Tax charge.
- you give your home away but continue to live there you must pay the new owner a commercial rent in order to avoid Inheritance Tax.

- you sell your home, then whatever amount from the sale proceeds you give to your children will be outside of Inheritance Tax provided you survive for seven years from the date of the gift. But if you then move in with them you will be exposed to an Income Tax charge on a 'pre-owned asset'.

- you give your home to your children and they move in with you, you will not have avoided Inheritance Tax as this will count as a 'gift with reservation of benefit'.

For couples, how you own your home determines the way in which it is passed on when you die, as follows:

Ownership	Beneficiary
Joint tenancy between spouses or civil partners	The survivor, automatically
Tenancy in common	In accordance with the will of the deceased, his or her share can be divided between the surviving spouse, partner and their children.

Business property

Transfers in lifetime or on death, subject to certain conditions, of eligible business assets and interests in businesses qualify for relief from Inheritance Tax. There are two rates:

- 100 per cent for:
  - unincorporated businesses;
  - all holdings of unquoted shares in qualifying companies;
  - unquoted shares, including those traded on the AIM market.
- 50 per cent for:
  - shares giving control of a quoted company;
  - land, buildings, machinery or plant used in a partnership or controlled company where the transferor is a partner or controlling shareholder.

Agricultural property

The reliefs applying to agricultural land and buildings are similar to those for business property. Subject to certain minimum ownership and use conditions, the two rates are again:

- 100 per cent for:
  - land and buildings where the transferor has vacant possession, or the right to obtain it, within 12 months;
  - agricultural property let for periods exceeding 12 months where letting commenced on or after 1 September 1995.
- 50 per cent for:
  - other qualifying property.

Rates of tax payable

Inheritance Tax is payable on:

- all transfers or gifts within three years of death; and
- on death.

The amount of Inheritance Tax payable is determined by the following table:

Cumulative chargeable transfers (£)	Rate (%)
0–325,000	0
Over 325,000	40*

* a reduced rate of 36 per cent is charged where at least 10 per cent of the net estate after taking off:

- all relief and expenditure; and
- the available nil rate band,

is left to charity.

The tax due on each chargeable gift or the value of your estate on death is dependent upon the cumulative value of all other chargeable transfers in the previous seven years.

Taper relief

A method of tapering relief applies where a donor dies within seven years of making a transfer. It is not the gift, but the amount of tax, that is reduced. The Inheritance Tax is worked out at the rate prevailing as at the date of death and then reduced in accordance with the following table:

Number of years between gift and death	% of IHT payable
Not more than 3	100
Between 3 and 4	80
Between 4 and 5	60
Between 5 and 6	40
Between 6 and 7	20

Gavin Wood, a bachelor, made his nephew, Rhys, a cash gift of £350,000 in May 2010. Gavin died in November 2015, leaving an estate of £400,000.

As Gavin did not survive for seven years, Rhys has to pay tax of £3,040 on his gift, calculated as follows:

	£
Cash gift	350,000
Less: Gavin's annual exemption limits for 2009/10 and 2010/11	6,000
	344,000
Less: Nil rate band at the date of Gavin's death	325,000
Tax payable on	19,000
Inheritance Tax thereon @ 40 per cent	7,600
Less: Taper Relief (60 per cent for surviving five years)	4,560
Tax payable	£3,040

It follows that there is no benefit of tapering relief where a PET, or the cumulative total of a number of PETs combined with any chargeable lifetime transfers, is within the limit of the nil rate band as at the date of death.

Transferable nil rate band

Any part of the nil rate band not used on the first death of a married couple or civil partners is not lost. It is available to all survivors of a marriage or civil partnership.

It does not matter when the first spouse of a marriage died; it can have occurred at any time. However, for civil partnerships, the first death must be later than 4 December 2005 when the Civil Partnership Act came into effect.

Any amount of the unused nil rate band can only be transferred from one spouse to the surviving spouse when their relationship is ended by the death of one of them. In cases of divorce where one party to the broken marriage subsequently dies, the relief will not be available.

On the death of the survivor:

- The percentage limit of the nil rate band applying on the death of the first spouse or civil partner that was unused is applied to the nil rate band when the survivor dies.

- The resulting amount is added to the survivor's own nil rate band.

Melvin Churchill died on 4 January 2008, leaving his estate of £200,000 to his wife, Eileen. She passed away on 10 December 2015, with an estate worth £600,000 divided between their four children.

When Melvin died, no part of the nil rate band at the time of £285,000 was used. Therefore, the nil rate band on Eileen's death is doubled to £650,000 and there is no Inheritance Tax to pay on her death.

Janice Timms died on 21 July 1996. Her estate amounted to £400,000. In her will she left legacies of £60,000 to each of her two children and the balance of her wealth to her husband, Colin. He passed away on 9 February 2016, worth £620,000 spread equally between the two children.

When Janice died the nil rate band was £200,000 of which 60 per cent (£120,000) was used against the legacies to her two children, leaving 40 per cent to transfer to Colin on his death earlier this year. Colin's nil rate band of £325,000 is increased by 40 per cent to £455,000, leaving Inheritance Tax at 40 per cent payable on £165,000.

Death

When someone dies, their assets pass into their estate to be administered by their personal representatives. Their main duties and responsibilities are to:

- gather in the assets of the deceased;
- settle their debts;
- pay out any legacies; and then
- distribute their remaining assets to the residuary beneficiaries.

It may also be necessary to complete a full Inheritance Tax Return and submit the form together with an application for a grant of:

- probate where there is a Will; or
- administration where there is no Will.

The Return must:

- be lodged within 12 months of the date of death; and
- include information about previous transfers and gifts in order that the amount of Inheritance Tax payable can be calculated.

In order to help your executors when the time comes, you are well advised to:

- let them know where your Will is kept;
- maintain up-to-date details of all your assets and where the supporting certificates and documents are stored; and
- keep complete records of your lifetime gifts.

Conrad Huxtable, a widower, died on 14 May 2015, leaving his entire estate to his son. He did not make any gifts in the seven years leading up to his death. His assets and unpaid bills at the time were:

Assets	Value	
	£	£
Home	360,000	
Household effects	4,000	
Car	3,000	
Building society account	20,000	
National Savings	8,000	
Individual Savings Accounts	13,000	
Bank current account	1,500	
Outstanding State Pension	540	
Cash	60	
		410,100
Less: Allowable deductions		
Funeral expenses	1,410	
Income tax	620	
Household bills	440	
Car repair	230	
		2,700
Net value of estate		£407,400
Inheritance Tax payable		
*On first £325,000		Nil
On next £82,400 at 40 per cent		32,960
		£32,960

* When Conrad's wife died her entire nil rate band was used in working out the tax on her estate.

The tax is payable out of Conrad Huxtable's estate by the executors of his Will.

Joshua Winterbottom, a bachelor, died on 9 January 2016, with an estate worth £620,000. Under his Will Joshua left legacies totalling £40,000 to a number of charities with the balance of his estate to his nieces and nephews.

The Inheritance Tax payable by his executors is £91,800 as follows:

	£	£
Value of Estate		620,000
Less: Legacies to charities	40,000	365,000
Nil rate band	325,000	
		255,000
Net estate		£255,000
Inheritance Tax at 36 per cent		£91,800

The rate of Inheritance Tax is 36 per cent as the charitable legacies of £40,000 are more than 10 per cent of Joshua's estate after taking off the nil rate band (£620,000 – £325,000 = £295,000 x 10 per cent = £29,500).

Sales at a loss

Relief from Inheritance Tax is due on certain assets sold within specified time limits after death for less than their values at the date of death:

- for quoted securities the period is one year; and
- in the case of land and buildings, the time limit extends to four years.

The relief is available to the 'appropriate person', namely the person who pays the tax. All sales by that person in the respective periods must be aggregated. As a result, losses can be restricted or eliminated by profits so that the relief may be reduced or even lost. When this type of relief is claimed, the sale proceeds, before selling expenses, are substituted for the valuation at death. The Inheritance Tax liability is then reworked.

Payment of tax

Primarily liable for the payment of Inheritance Tax are:

- the transferor in respect of chargeable lifetime gifts; and
- the personal representatives on death.

Personal representatives can draw on funds held in a deceased's bank and building society accounts solely for the purpose of paying any Inheritance Tax that is due before the Grant of Probate can be issued. The payment dates for Inheritance Tax are:

Type of charge	Due date for payment
Chargeable lifetime gifts	Six months after the end of the month in which the gift was made
PETs that become taxable on death, and the charge on death	Six months after the end of the month in which death itself occurred

There is an option to pay the tax due on some types of asset by 10 equal annual instalments. For lifetime transfers that are, or become, chargeable, this instalment option is only available if the tax is borne by the transferee. The first amount is, however, payable on the normal due date.

The assets concerned are:

- land and buildings;
- controlling shareholdings;
- unquoted shares, subject to certain conditions; and
- businesses.

Where the relevant asset is disposed of during the instalment paying period, all the outstanding instalments of Inheritance Tax become immediately payable.

Interest and penalties

Interest is chargeable on Inheritance Tax liabilities from the due date until the date of payment. At the time of going to print, the rate of interest is 3 per cent. Any repayment of tax or interest thereon carries interest presently at the much lower rate of 0.5 per cent for the period from the date it was paid until it is refunded.

Where the instalment option is in effect, no interest is charged on the outstanding instalments of Inheritance Tax, except on:

- land and buildings that do not qualify for either business or agricultural property reliefs; and

- shares and securities in investment companies.

As with your Tax Return, there are penalties for late or incorrect Returns, delays, negligence or fraud as well as the late payment of Inheritance Tax.

Excepted estates

Where no Inheritance Tax is due:

- the estate is usually referred to as an 'excepted estate'; and

- a simpler form can be submitted as part of the probate process.

The estate will generally be an excepted estate if:

- it is of low value, in other words under the threshold for Inheritance Tax – £325,000 for 2015/16; or

- it is classed as an exempt estate. This is where the deceased leaves everything to a spouse, civil partner or charity.

But, in some cases, a full Inheritance Tax Return may still be required even if there is no tax to pay:

- depending on the assets and debts of an estate; and

- the history of lifetime giving.

Intestacy

If you die without having made a Will, your estate will be distributed under the Intestate Estate Rules. There are two tables:

- one for an unmarried individual; and
- the other for a person with a surviving spouse.

The intestacy rules for individuals who die domiciled in England and Wales are as follows:

Unmarried individual	Division
Survived by Children or grandchildren Parents Brothers and sisters Half-brothers and half-sisters Grandparents Uncles and aunts The Crown	The total estate is shared in the following order of priority, to the exclusion of all others

Married individual with surviving spouse	Division
(1) Estate amounts to less than £250,000.	All to spouse
(2) Estate exceeds £250,000 and there are children.	Spouse is entitled to the personal belongings, the first £250,000 and half the remainder. The balance is shared between the children
(3) There are no children.	All to spouse

The spouse must survive the intestate individual by 28 days to become entitled under the intestacy rules.

Civil partners, and the children of a civil partnership, benefit under the intestacy rules in the same way as spouses and the children of a marriage.

Legacies

If you are fortunate enough to receive a legacy from a member of your family or a friend:

- Any Inheritance Tax on a legacy will be accounted for by the executors before you receive it.
- You do not have to pay either Income Tax or Capital Gains Tax on a legacy.
- It does not need to be reported on your annual Tax Return.

How to save on Inheritance Tax

Tax Saver

Here are some hints and tips on how to minimize the impact of Inheritance Tax on both your lifetime giving and the value of your estate on death.

- First and foremost, make a Will. Otherwise your estate will devolve under the intestacy laws and maybe not in the way that you want. This is particularly relevant for co-habitees who have no entitlement where there is no Will.

- Make sure you keep your Will up to date.

- To make life as easy as possible for your executors keep a file or register with up-to-date information of all your assets and where any certificates or documents are kept.

- Maintain a record of your lifetime gifts.

- Remember that gifts and transfers, during lifetime and on death, between husbands/wives and civil partners are exempt from Inheritance Tax.

- Whenever you can afford to do so, make use of the various exemptions detailed in this chapter. By giving throughout your life you will significantly cut down on the amount of Inheritance Tax payable on your estate.

- The 'normal expenditure out of income' exemption is ideal for dealing with the payment of regular premiums on life policies written in Trust for younger generations. As the policy proceeds pass to them free of tax this is, in effect, a substitute for the payment of an Inheritance Tax liability on death, which cannot otherwise be avoided.

- Non-exempt gifts or transfers should be made as early as possible to increase your chances of surviving the seven-year period. Make immediately chargeable gifts – for example transfers into settlement – before those that are potentially exempt.

- Give assets that do not qualify for relief before those that do.

- If possible give assets with low values so that they appreciate in the hands of the recipient and outside your estate.

- Maybe you could rearrange some of your investments so that you can take advantage of the generous reliefs for agricultural or business property. Companies whose shares are quoted on AIM and which are trading companies count as unquoted for business property relief purposes.

- Gifts and legacies to charities are exempt from Inheritance Tax. If you donate at least 10 per cent of your net estate to charity, the rate of Inheritance Tax payable on the balance comes down from 40 per cent to 36 per cent.

- Consider restricting the chargeable legacies for the next generations to an amount equivalent to the nil rate band for Inheritance Tax, leaving the remainder of your estate to your spouse or civil partner. He or she can then make gifts and hopefully live for a further seven years.

- In the two years after death, consider the use of a Deed of Variation in order to utilize any available exemptions that would otherwise be lost.

Budget measures

18

Against a background of:

- challenging economic statistics and forecasts; and
- the June 2016 EU referendum,

the Chancellor still managed to spring a few surprises in his March 2016 Budget statement.

The most striking measures he announced were:

- For 2017/18, increases in the personal allowance to £11,500 and the amount of income taxable at the basic rate to £33,500.
- Cuts in both rates of Capital Gains Tax starting from 2016/17.
- The launch of a new Lifetime ISA from April 2017 for adults under age 40, allowing them to save up to £4,000 per annum coupled with a 25 per cent government bonus.

This chapter details the tax changes effective from 6 April 2016 which were:

- already in the pipeline;
- in the post-election July 2015 Budget;
- set out in the Autumn 2015 Statement; or
- announced by the Chancellor in his 2016 Budget.

This is followed by a summary of proposed measures that will not take effect until 6 April 2017 or later.

2016/17 personal allowances

	£
Personal	
all individuals	11,000*
Married couples	
born before 6 April 1935	8,355**/***
minimum amount	3,220***
Transferable marriage allowance	1,100****
Income limits	
for personal allowance	100,000
for married couple's allowance	27,700
Relief for blind person (each)	2,290

*	the personal allowance reduces at the rate of £1 for every £2 of income in excess of £100,000.
**	the married couple's allowance comes down by £1 for every £2 of income above the income limit of £27,700.
***	indicates allowances where tax relief is restricted to 10 per cent.
****	available to spouses/civil partners born after 5 April 1935.

Tax rates and bands for 2016/17

Band of taxable income (£)	Rate of tax (%)	Tax on band (£)	Cumulative tax (£)
0–32,000	20	6,400	6,400
32,001–150,000	40	47,200	53,600
Over 150,000	45		

Scottish rate of Income Tax

From 6 April 2016, if you live in Scotland:

- you will pay the 10 per cent Scottish rate of Income Tax;
- your UK Income Tax rate will come down by 10 per cent; and
- your April 2016 tax code will begin with the letter 'S'.

The Scottish rate does not apply to:

- savings income, such as bank or building society interest; or
- dividends.

Overall, your annual income tax bill will be the same as taxpayers living in the rest of the UK. But some of the income tax gathered in by HMRC under the Scottish rate will be passed on to the Scottish Government. The balance will go to the UK Government.

Personal Savings Allowance

Starting from 2016/17 a new tax free Personal Savings Allowance is introduced as follows:

Type of taxpayer	Amount of tax free savings income (£)
Basic rate	1,000
Higher rate	500

Additional rate taxpayers do not receive any allowance.
As a consequence of this new measure:

- many individuals will receive all their savings interest tax free; and
- banks and building societies will no longer deduct tax at source on interest they pay.

Savings income

From 2016/17 a zero rate still applies to the first £5,000 of taxable savings income. But this zero rate is only available on any part of your taxable savings income:

- of up to £5,000; and
- after taking off your personal allowance.

Dividend income

From 2016/17 the notional tax credit attaching to dividends:

- is abolished; and
- replaced by a nil rate band of £5,000 on dividend income.

The rates of tax payable on dividends above the £5,000 allowance are as follows:

For dividends otherwise taxable at:	Rate (%)
Basic rate	7.5
Higher rate	32.5
Additional rate	38.1

Rates of National Insurance Contributions for 2016/17

Class 1   Contributions for employees

Contributions levied on weekly earnings above £155 that do not exceed £827

Standard rate	12%
Contracted out	10.6%

Earnings threshold

Weekly	£155
Monthly	£672
Annually	£8,060

Upper earnings limit

Weekly	£827
Monthly	£3,583
Annually	£43,000

Contributions levied on all weekly earnings in excess of £827	2%
Reduced rate for married women and widows with a valid Election Certificate on earnings below upper earnings limit	5.85%
Men and women over State Pension age	Nil

Class 2   Contributions for the self-employed

Weekly flat rate	£2.80
Small earnings exception	£5,965

Class 3   Voluntary contributions

Weekly rate	£14.10

Class 4   Contributions for the self-employed

On profits between £8,060 and £43,000	9%
On profits in excess of £43,000	2%

Rates of Child Tax Credits and Working Tax Credits for 2016/17

	£
Child Tax Credit	
Family element	545
Child element (each child)	2,780
Disabled child element	3,140
Severe disability element	1,275
Working Tax Credit	
Basic entitlement	1,960
Additional couples and lone parent element	2,010
30-hour element	810
Disability element	2,970
Severe disability element	1,275
Childcare element	
Maximum eligible cost for two or more children	£300 per week
Maximum eligible cost for one child	£175 per week
Percentage of eligible cost covered	70%

Tax credits will taper away at a rate of 41 per cent for each £1 of family income over the first income threshold of £6,420 (£16,105 when no Working Tax Credit is claimed).

The amount that a claimant's income can increase for tax credit purposes without any reduction in entitlement comes down from £5,000 to £2,500.

Benefits-in-kind

From 2016/17:

- Trivial benefits-in-kind costing no more than £50 will be exempt from tax and need not be reported to HMRC.
- The £8,500 annual income threshold exempting employees from income tax on most benefits or perks is abolished.

Tax-Free Childcare Scheme

From early 2017 a new scheme will be available for working families, whether:

- employed; or
- self-employed,

to help with the cost of childcare.

To qualify, parents:

- must be in work; and
- earn just over £100 a week; but
- not more than £100,000 a year.

For every 80p contributed by eligible families the Government will put in 20p, thereby providing support of up to £2,000 a year for each child.

The scheme will be available to children up to:

- age 12; or
- age 17 for those with disabilities.

The scheme was originally set to be introduced in the autumn of 2015. However, the launch date had to be postponed because of a legal challenge.

Company car and fuel benefits

From 6 April 2016:

- The taxable benefit for all cars increases by 2 per cent up to a maximum of 37 per cent.
- The multiplier to be applied in working out the taxable benefit on fuel used for private motoring in a company car increases from £22,100 to £22,200.

Company van and fuel benefits

From 6 April 2016:

- Where your employer provides you with a company van, without any unrestricted use, and no matter the age or size of the van, the fixed amount on which you are taxed increases to £3,170.
- The taxable benefit for personal mileage goes up to £598.

Employee share ownership

An individual lifetime limit of £100,000 is introduced for arrangements made after 16 March 2016 where the gains are free of Capital Gains Tax because of employee shareholder status.

Pensions

From 6 April 2016 the annual allowance for pension saving will be tapered for individuals with earned income exceeding £150,000 (including pension contributions). The rate of taper is £1 for every £2 by which income is more than £150,000. The maximum reduction is £30,000. Accordingly, the current annual allowance of £40,000 can come down to £10,000.

Buy-to-let

With effect from 6 April 2016 the 10 per cent wear and tear allowance is abolished. In its place comes a new relief allowing residential landlords to deduct the actual costs of replacing furnishings.

Claims to capital allowances continue to apply for furnished holiday accommodation.

Rent-a-room

From 6 April 2016 the tax-free income you can receive from renting out spare rooms in your home for residential accommodation goes up from £4,250 to £7,500 per annum.

Individual Savings Accounts

For 2016/17 the maximum annual amount that can be invested by all qualifying individuals remains unchanged at £15,240.

Junior Individual Savings Accounts and Child Trust Funds

From 2016/17 the maximum investment limit for both types of account stays at £4,080 per annum.

Value Added Tax

The Value Added Tax registration threshold is increased with effect from 1 April 2016 from taxable turnover of £82,000 to £83,000. The cancellation of registration limit goes up from £80,000 to £81,000.

New fuel scale charges for businesses with prescribed accounting periods starting on or after 1 May 2016 have been issued.

Capital Gains Tax

For 2016/17:

- The Capital Gains Tax exemption limit remains at £11,100.
- The 18 per cent and 28 per cent rates of tax come down to 10 per cent and 20 per cent. However, this tax reduction does not extend to tax payable on the disposal of residential property that does not qualify for private residence relief; for example, buy-to-let.

Entrepreneurs' Relief is extended to the disposal of ordinary shares purchased by investors after 16 March 2016 in unlisted trading companies. There is no requirement for an investor:

- to be an officer or employee of the company; and
- hold more than 5 per cent of the shares and voting rights in it.

The shares must be held for at least three years, starting from 6 April 2016. The rate of Capital Gains Tax payable is 10 per cent on qualifying lifetime gains up to £10 million.

Inheritance Tax

The nil rate band is unchanged at £325,000.

Looking into the future

The measures so far announced but not taking effect until at least 6 April 2017 are:

Measure	Date of Introduction
The personal allowance will rise to £11,500.	6 April 2017
The limit of income taxable at the basic rate goes up to £33,500.	6 April 2017
Two new allowances for trading and property income of £1,000 each will be introduced. These have primarily been designed to ease the compliance burden for those individuals with small amounts of taxable profits from either source of income.	6 April 2017
The annual ISA subscription limit increases to £20,000.	6 April 2017
Taxpayers under 40 years old will be able to take out a new Lifetime ISA into which they can save up to £4,000 per annum until age 50. The Government will make an additional 25 per cent contribution to the savings in the account. The funds in the Lifetime ISA must either be used to assist with the purchase of a first home costing up to £450,000 or withdrawn tax free after a taxpayer reaches age 60. Failing this, the Government bonus, plus any interest or growth on it, must be repaid. A 5 per cent levy will also be charged. Monies saved through a Lifetime ISA will count towards the annual ISA subscription limit.	6 April 2017
Non-domiciled taxpayers will be regarded as domiciled in the UK for all taxes once they have been a UK resident for 15 out of the previous 20 tax years. As a result they will become liable to UK tax on their worldwide income and gains.	6 April 2017
New rates for zero or low emission cars have been set for 2017/18 and 2018/19.	6 April 2017

Measure	Date of Introduction
The amount of tax relief on mortgage interest and other finance costs for individuals investing in buy-to-let residential property is to be restricted to the basic rate of tax. This measure is to be phased in gradually over three years.	6 April 2017
A 'family home allowance', eventually worth £175,000 for each person, is to be added to the existing £325,000 nil rate band for Inheritance Tax. This allowance will start at £100,000 in 2017/18, increasing to £175,000 by 2020/21. By 5 April 2021 this measure will enable individuals to pass on assets worth up to £500,000, including a family home, without any liability at all to Inheritance Tax. For married couples and civil partners this increases to £1 million.	6 April 2017
Class 2 National Insurance Contributions for the self-employed are to be abolished.	6 April 2018
The taxable benefit for all company cars goes up by 3 per cent, subject to a maximum of 37 per cent.	6 April 2019
The 3 per cent supplement on diesel cars is to be removed so that they will be subject to the same level of tax as petrol cars.	6 April 2021

APPENDICES

1. HMRC (Revenue) explanatory booklets and help sheets

Booklets

No	Title
IR 115	Paying for Childcare: Getting help from your employer
480	Expenses and Benefits: A tax guide
490	Employee Travel – A Tax and NIC's Guide
SE 1	Setting Up in Business
RK BK 1	Keeping Records for Your Tax Return
HMRC 1	HMRC Decisions: What to do if you disagree
RDR 1	Guidance Note: Residence, domicile and the remittance basis
RDR 3	Guidance Note: Statutory residence test
WTC 1	Child Tax Credit and Working Tax Credit: An introduction
WTC 2	Child Tax Credit and Working Tax Credit: A guide
WTC 5	Working Tax Credit – Help With the Costs of Childcare
WTC 6	Other Types of Help You Could Get
WTC 7	Tax Credit Penalties

Help sheets

General

HS305	Employee Shares and Securities – Further Guidance
HS320	Gains on UK Life Assurance policies
HS325	Other Taxable Income
HS341	Enterprise Investment Scheme: Income Tax relief
HS342	Charitable Giving

Employment

HS201	Vouchers, Credit Cards and Tokens
HS202	Living Accommodation
HS203	Car Benefits and Car Fuel Benefits
HS204	Limit on Income Tax Reliefs
HS207	Non-Taxable Payments or Benefits for Employees
HS208	Payslips and Coding Notices
HS210	Assets Provided for Private Use
HS211	Employment: Residence and domicile issues

Self-employment

HS220	More than One Business
HS222	How to Calculate Your Taxable Profits
HS227	Losses
HS229	Information from Your Accounts
HS252	Capital Allowances and Balancing Charges

2. Flat-rate allowances for special clothing and the upkeep of tools – 2015/16

(1) Fixed rate for all occupations	£
Agricultural	100
Clothing	60
Forestry	100
Quarrying	100
Brass and copper	120
Precious metals	100
Food	60
Glass	80
Railways (non-crafts people)	100
Uniformed prison officers	80
Uniformed bank and building society employees	60
Uniformed police officers up to and including Chief Inspector	140
Uniformed fire fighters and fire officers	80

(2) Variable rate depending on category of occupation	£
Seamen	140/165
Iron mining	100/120
Iron and steel	60/80/140
Aluminium	60/80/120/140
Engineering	60/80/120/140
Shipyards	60/80/100/140
Vehicles	60/80/140
Particular engineering	60/80/120/140
Constructional engineering	60/80/100/140
Electrical and electricity supply	60/120
Textiles and textile printing	80/120
Leather	60/80
Printing	60/100/140
Building materials	60/80/120
Wood and furniture	60/100/120/140
Building	60/80/120/140
Heating	100/120
Public service	60/80
Healthcare	60/100/140

NOTE: The allowances are only available to manual workers who have to bear the cost of upkeep of tools and special clothing. Other employees, such as office staff, cannot claim them.

3. HMRC (VAT) notices and leaflets

No	Title
700	The VAT Guide
700/1	Should I Be Registered for VAT?
700/11	Cancelling Your Registration
700/12	How to Fill in and Submit Your VAT Return
700/18	Relief from VAT on Bad Debts
700/21	Keeping Records and Accounts
700/41	Late Registration Penalty
700/42	Misdeclaration and Repeated Misdeclaration Penalties
700/43	Default Interest
700/45	How to Correct VAT Errors and Make Adjustments or Claims
700/50	Default Surcharge
700/58	Treatment of VAT Repayment Returns and VAT Repayment Supplement
700/60	Payments on Account
700/62	Self Billing
700/63	Electronic Invoicing
700/64	Motoring Expenses
700/65	Business Entertainment
727	Retail Schemes
731	Cash Accounting
732	Annual Accounting
733	Flat Rate Scheme for Small Businesses

4. Rates of National Insurance Contributions for 2015/16

CLASS 1 *Contributions for employees*

Contributions levied on all weekly earnings above £155 but that do not exceed £815:

Standard rate:	12%
Contracted out:	10.6%

Earnings threshold

Weekly:	£155
Monthly:	£672
Annual:	£8,060

Upper earnings limit

Weekly:	£815
Monthly:	£3,532
Annual:	£42,385

Contributions levied on all weekly earnings in excess of £805:	2%
Reduced rate for married women and widows with a valid election certificate on earnings below upper earnings limit:	5.85%
Rates for men and women over state pensionable age:	Nil

CLASS 2 *Contributions for the self-employed*

Weekly flat rate:	£2.80
Small earnings exception:	£5,965

CLASS 3 *Voluntary contributions*

Weekly rate:	£14.10

CLASS 4 *Contributions for the self-employed*

On profits between £8,060 and £42,385:	9%
On profits in excess of £42,385:	2%

5. Social Security benefits

Taxable

Incapacity Benefit after the first 28 weeks (1) (2)
Employment and Support Allowance (contribution-based) (3)
Industrial Death Benefit Pensions
Invalidity Allowance Paid with State Pension
Jobseeker's Allowance
State Retirement Pension (1)
Carer's Allowance (1)
Statutory Adoption Pay
Statutory Maternity and Paternity Pay
Statutory Shared Parental Pay
Statutory Sick Pay
Widows and Widowers Bereavement Benefits

Non-taxable

Incapacity Benefit for the first 28 weeks (1) (2)
Employment and Support Allowance (income-related) (3)
Income Support
Maternity Allowance
Child Benefit (4)
Child Tax Credit
Child Dependency Additions
Guardian's Allowance
Christmas Bonus for Pensioners
Industrial Injury Benefits
Disability Living Allowance
Personal Independence Payment (5)
Severe Disablement Allowance
Bereavement Payment (Lump Sum)
Universal Credit (6)
Housing Benefit (income-related)
War Disablement Pensions
Social Fund Payments
Attendance Allowance

Vaccine Damage (Lump Sum)
Cold Weather and Winter Fuel Payments
Pension Credit
Working Tax Credit

Notes

1 Child dependency additions to these benefits are not taxable.

2 Existing claimants on 27 October 2008.

3 Replaced Incapacity Benefit for new claimants from 27 October 2008.

4 Except for those liable to the High Income Tax Charge.

5 Replaced Disability Living Allowance for new claimants from 8 April 2013.

6 Is gradually being introduced to replace some existing benefits.

6. Rates of main Social Security benefits for 2015/16

Weekly rate from 06/04/2015 onwards	£
Taxable	
Retirement pensions	
Single person	115.95
Married couples: both contributors – each	115.95
Wife not contributor – addition	69.50
Age addition (over 80) – each	0.25
Bereavement benefits	
Bereavement allowance/widow's pension – maximum	112.55
Widowed parent's allowance	112.55
Jobseeker's allowance	
Age 18 to 24	57.90
Age 25 or over	73.10
Couple both 18 or over	114.85
Incapacity benefit	
Long-term	105.35
Increase for age:	
– higher rate	11.15
– lower rate	6.20
Short-term (under pension age):	
– lower rate	79.45
– higher rate	94.05
(over pension age):	
– lower rate	101.10
– higher rate	105.35
Statutory sick pay	
Standard rate (weekly earnings threshold £112)	88.45
Statutory maternity, paternity and adoption pay	
Rate (weekly earnings threshold £112)	139.58
Non-taxable	
Maternity allowance	
Standard rate	139.58
Child benefit	
Only or eldest child (couple or lone parent)	20.70
Each other child	13.70
Attendance allowance	
Higher rate	82.30
Lower rate	55.10

7. Main dates of the Self Assessment calendar 6 April 2016 to 5 April 2017

Date	What happens	Who is affected
6 April 2016	2015/16 Tax Returns sent out by HMRC.	Taxpayers who need to fill in an annual Tax Return.
31 July 2016	Second payment on account due for 2015/16.	Those taxpayers who make regular half-yearly payments on account.
1 August 2016	First tax geared penalty levied for failing to submit a 2014/15 Tax Return before this date.	Taxpayers who have not yet completed and sent back their 2014/15 Tax Returns.
2 August 2016	Further 5% late payment penalty on tax still outstanding for 2014/15.	Late payers of tax still due for 2014/15.
31 October 2016	Filing deadline for completing and returning 2015/16 paper Tax Returns.	Taxpayers who want HMRC to: • calculate their tax for 2015/16; • collect tax owing for 2015/16 of less than £3,000 through their code number in 2017/18.
31 December 2016	Non-mandatory filing deadline for 2015/16 online Tax Returns.	Online filers who want HMRC to collect tax owing for 2015/16 of less than £3,000 through their code number in 2017/18.
31 January 2017	Filing deadline for 2015/16 online Tax Returns. Payment date for the balance of tax due for 2015/16 and the first payment on account for 2016/17.	Taxpayers sent a 2015/16 Tax Return. Taxpayers who need to settle either of these liabilities.
1 February 2017	First penalty notices issued for the late filing of a 2015/16 Tax Return.	Taxpayers who were sent a 2015/16 Tax Return.
3 March 2017	First 5% late payment penalty imposed for failing to pay tax due by 31 January 2017 and still outstanding on 2 March 2017.	Late payers of tax for 2015/16.

INDEX

Note: page numbers in *italic* indicate figures and tables